Teaching Tennis

Vol. 1

The Fundamentals of the Game

Martin van Daalen

To order additional copies of this book, contact:
Xlibris Corporation
1-888-795-4274
www.Xlibris.com
Orders@Xlibris.com
97166

CONTENTS

FOR MY PARENTS

They always encouraged me to be the best
I could be at whatever I attempted to do.

FOREWORD

By Lynne Rolley
Former Director, Women's Tennis USTA

You might find yourself in a position of wanting to learn tennis or ensure you are on track with your game. Or it might be that you want to enhance your teaching as a coach to guide your students through their development. Martin van Daalen has captured the entire process in his book, *Teaching Tennis*. He will enable you, as a reader, to coach yourself or others in all the fundamentals that can lead you or your child to become a sound tennis player. Besides the basics of the game, you can learn all about the technical, tactical, physical, and mental aspects of teaching tennis. His clear and concise explanations come from years of leadership in coaching players, coaches, and parents and have proven to be successful. He has done his work for you. Read it and use it to your benefit!

By Rodney Harmon
Former Director, Men's Tennis USTA

Martin van Daalen is one of the finest coaches in tennis today. He is blessed with an uncanny ability to not only quickly and correctly breakdown a stroke or playing sequence but also offer a clear, concise plan to correct the problem. He loves the game and is happiest working with players in helping them reach their full potential. I have known Martin for over fifteen years, and I am proud to call him a friend. We worked together, for a number of years, with the USTA High Performance Men's Program, and I was always impressed with his approach to teaching and his work ethic.

His knowledge and experience of coaching have been shaped for over thirty-five years by his passion for the game and take-charge attitude that still drives him today. I have learned so much from Martin about coaching and developing players, and he is always ready to share his experience with any coach who has a question or a problem. Besides his coaching ability, his special gift is his willingness to spend time with the players to help them mature as people. Often, a personal coach spends more time with a particular player than the parents, especially as the player matures and goes on the road playing tournaments. The coach can be of tremendous influence to how the player grows up, often during a stressful time of their lives. I have watched Martin spend time with players, discussing the game of life and the importance of hard work, integrity, honesty, and kindness to others.

This book will give you a great insight into concepts, drills, and patterns that will develop players of all levels. Martin's knowledge and experience of the game spans such a wide range from players just starting to play the game to those competing on the ATP/WTA tours. He is a clear thinker, and his book has information that you can use today or tomorrow to help improve your player or yourself. I have read this book a number of times, and I refer to it many times as I train my students. This book has helped me, and I know it will do the same for you!

Martin van Daalen

Martin van Daalen (age twenty-two)

PREFACE

It was my dad who introduced me to the game of tennis when I was ten years old. That summer, he took my brother and me to the local tennis club and showed us how to play the game. We practiced together often until we became good enough to compete in tournaments. I played my first tournament when I was twelve and lost to the number 1 seed. Even though I was very upset, it was at that moment I decided I wanted to be good at this wonderful sport of tennis.

As a junior, I had a lot of good players to practice with. I also had some great coaches who taught me the basics of the game. Having an older brother to compete with helped as well. We would spend afternoons at the club playing singles and doubles matches against each other. There was a great tennis environment with players of every age joining in.

Growing up in Holland, I played for most part in the summer because the winters were too cold. Private lessons were expensive, and I was fortunate to receive one or two hours of instruction a week. It took over an hour of travel each way to get there. Practice was never boring to me, so I never minded the travel. From a young age, I was very independent in taking charge of my tennis. I made my own tournament schedule and took care of all the entries myself. I couldn't wait for the new tournament schedule to arrive each spring and usually had my plan ready for the year that same afternoon!

Sometimes, my parents drove me to the tournaments, but often, I would take the bus or train to get there. I started making notes of my training, my improvements, and the players I played. Taking notes helped me remember the things that went well and what to improve and the specifics about matches and players. I became my own coach at an early stage.

I started getting much more serious about my tennis game around the age of sixteen. Winning matches and becoming the junior 18-and-under club champion sure helped my confidence. With the limited coaching hours, compared to training today, I had to be resourceful to coach myself by reading more tennis books and making notes of my practice. I also started to do a little coaching on the side to pay for some of the traveling and to have a little extra pocket money.

After high school, I attended two years of technical college (mechanical engineering) before I realized how much I missed tennis. Little did I know that the mechanical engineering background would help me tremendously in my coaching career.

Europe has professional training for coaches, and I assigned myself the goal of becoming the best coach I could possibly be. The two years' training was extensive and detailed in teaching tennis. Part of the course is an internship working at a club, under the tutelage of an experienced instructor and coach from the teaching program. Together with the other student coaches, we had to learn by trial and error, how to coach students of different levels. The learning process of teaching and evaluating each other proved to be an excellent experience and training in becoming a coach.

When I was twenty-one, I was drafted in the national army of the Netherlands for sixteen months and stationed in Germany. Being in the army made me tougher and much more assertive in dealing with others. With the rank of a sergeant, I learned how to lead others with a calm and determined demeanor. (Later on, I would help organize the first boot camp for top junior tennis players in the United States at the U.S. Marine Corps headquarters in San Diego, directed by Sgt. Maj. Keith Williams.)

After the draft, I continued the coaches' training course and, at the age of twenty-one, became the youngest national coach in the Netherlands at that time. Even then, I started working on a book of training plans for technique, tactics, mental, and physical training. Taking ownership and initiative in my future job was an early asset in my development as a teacher and a coach. After finishing the second coaching course for advanced players, I was working at three different clubs with most of the top players in the eastern part of the Holland and was (playing) captain of the top team for many years.

I decided I needed more international experience and wrote the famous coach Harry Hopman to request an intern coaching position at his academy in Clearwater, Florida. The Dutch Tennis Federation granted me a leave of absence to go there for three months to learn new coaching methods. It was a great experience to coach and play with the world's best players at the time. Some of the top players that trained there were John McEnroe, Bjorn Borg, Vitas Gerulaitis, and many other great players from those days. It was a very busy place with up to 250 players training there each week. I trained there myself with Paul McNamee, Kathy Horvath, Jimmy Brown, Andrea Yeager, and many others. Later, I returned to Holland to continue my work with the federation. I applied a lot of the new coaching techniques in working with the players and in playing tournaments.

A few years later, when visiting the United States, I was offered a job at the tennis resort called Saddlebrook. They had recently taken over the program from Harry Hopman, who had passed away the previous year. Working there for six and a half years was very interesting and educational. My task was to work with a variety of top junior players and professionals: Jared Palmer, Ty Tucker, Mary Pierce, Jennifer Capriati, Mark Kratzmann, Shuzo Matsuoka, Pete Sampras, Jeff Tarango, Jim Courier, and too many others to name. During this time, I took on a number of coaching opportunities that meant traveling on the road with top juniors, pro-level players, and federations including the USTA. One of those opportunities was in Japan, working at a club and coaching juniors of the Japanese federation. It was a very rich period of experience in learning to cope with all the various international players, customs, and styles of play.

I was offered and accepted a job in Amsterdam as a head coach in a newly established academy and was in charge of all the training. I started with only six students. The academy grew rapidly, and within three years, I had forty-five students. It was a rewarding achievement to build this academy from the ground up. It was a joy to work and develop this talented group of players. One major accomplishment that I am very proud of during this time was winning the top national league for three ears in a row.

My next position, as director of Women's Tennis for the Dutch Tennis Federation, taught me a lot about management and, unfortunately, about the politics in tennis. Even though I did not enjoy this position as much, it was a great learning tool in dealing with players, coaches, parents, and board members.

After this position ended, I took on a very promising junior, Michelle Gerards, to train her privately for the year. She made tremendous progress and, at the age of thirteen, won the national indoor championship for 18 and under. I was sad that I was not able to continue her development when I was invited to join the USTA player development program as a national coach and coordinator of the south region (southern nine states).

I worked for the USTA for eleven and a half years in various positions. When I first started there, I worked under Tom Gullickson (director of coaching) and, later, Lynne Rolley (director of women's tennis) and Rodney Harmon (director of men's tennis). I was always involved with the development of young top junior players. Some of those players were Ashley Harkleroad, Alex Kuznetsov, Chase Buchanan, Rhyne Williams, and Ryan Harrison, to name a few. At one point, I was very involved in changing the ranking system in the United States to a point system similar to the one used by the ATP, WTA, and ITF junior ranking. It made sense that juniors in the United States learned to play for points just as they do on the international scene. After some opposition to the idea, it finally became a fact and is now an intricate part of the junior competition and development in the United States. The new system sparked the competitive spirit of many players, and they began playing a lot more matches. In addition, it also allows players to check and calculate their own ranking via the Internet. As a national coach, I traveled with juniors to national and international events. The grand slam junior tournaments are always the main goal of the year. When the USTA commenced their training program in Boca Raton, I was in charge of the player development group of coaches on the men's side. I oversaw the coaches and the development of the players at the academy, and I assisted with the coaching education of the national men's coaches. At this time, I am working privately with players in the United States.

The fundamentals of the game are an important part to the development of every player. So if you are a coach, player, or parent, this is a great tool in teaching yourself, or others, how to learn this game from the beginning. May you have as much fun reading it as I had writing it!

INTRODUCTION

TEACHING TENNIS is a comprehensive book for players, coaches, and parents to learn about the basics of tennis, how to teach tennis, and how to solve problems concerning all aspects of the game. It is the first of three books, with volume 1 containing the fundamentals of the game. The other two books contain subjects for advanced and professional levels of play.

This first book explains, in detail, how to instruct yourself or others while avoiding some of the pitfalls in learning the game. It shows the progression of the various subjects with many examples of drills and exercises. Players are able to follow this book step-by-step and improve their game with tips and photo sequences of the different strokes. This book is a first step for coaches to improve their knowledge and teaching skills when working with players. *Teaching Tennis* is an extensive how-to book for coaches that illustrates the fundamentals of teaching and coaching in progression. It includes a large section on problem solving with examples of common errors, error detection and corrections. Coaches are able to use it as a teaching guide to develop players with a philosophy and methodology to coaching with enhanced techniques. Parents can use this book to either assist their children with coaching or use it as a reference or handbook in solving many issues that arise in the development of tennis players.

AGES 8 & UNDER

AGE	COURT SIZE	RACQUET	BALL	NET HEIGHT	SCORING
8 years and under	36' x 18'	up to 23"	foam or very low compression	2' 9"	best of 3 games 1st to 7 points wins game first to win 2 games wins match

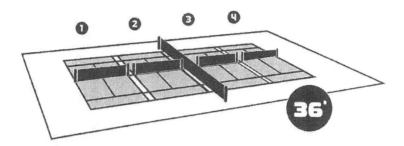

AGES 10 & UNDER

AGE	COURT SIZE	RACQUET	BALL	NET HEIGHT	SCORING
10 years and under	60' x 21' singles 60' x 27' doubles	up to 25"	low compression	3'	best of 2 sets of 1st to 4 games with 3rd set 1st to 7 points

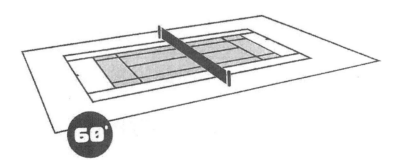

GETTING STARTED

Tennis is a fun game that can be played by anyone at any age, and it is not as difficult as it seems. To get started playing tennis, there are a lot of programs and many public parks available to play and practice. Before you begin, consider the following:

Equipment

The rackets should be the proper size. A good way to measure the length is to have the students hold the racket by the handle straight down to the ground. The top of the racket should touch the ground or be just above. The grips vary in size as well. When holding the grip, there should be a small space between the fingers and the base of the thumb. If the fingers touch, the grip is too small. There are many types of string available, but starting off, a nylon string is sufficient. As the players become more proficient, you will notice the strings break more frequently. String tension is a matter of experience over time. Most junior programs carry the proper rackets in the pro shop, and the local pro can be very helpful in choosing the right one for your child. Shoes and apparel are readily available in every sports shop. Proper shoes for the surface can be important so you don't slip. Clay court shoes are different from indoor and hard-court shoes.

Programs

There are many local programs you can find in your neighborhood. The Internet is a good way to find them listed with the various programs. Here are some for you to think about:

1 – Quick Start (see opposite page)
Many tennis clubs offer beginning tennis for young children. One popular program is Quick Start. Quick Start is a rapidly growing tennis program that focuses on beginning players from age four and up. This program is designed to help children enjoy tennis and be successful at an early age. The courts are smaller and the nets are lower. The juniors play with lighter and smaller rackets and foam balls. It is truly amazing to see how fast they

learn to play the ball back and forth at that age. I have seen Quick Start tournaments organized with great success and participation. The rackets are not expensive, and you would do well, as parents, to ask your local pro for advice on this equipment. There are complete quick start equipment sets available from many different racket companies.

2 – Junior Programs
Every good club has a junior development program (see chapter Info and Web Pages). Some might be better than others. The best way to find out is to ask the parents. Or even better, ask the juniors themselves how they like it! Try to find a program that not only gives the kids instruction but also provides them some time to play on their own. Most junior programs start at five or six years old and preferably should not last longer than an hour of instruction for them to have some time to play by themselves. Having a decent-size program with at least fifteen to thirty kids helps them to compete in matches with plenty of practice partners.

3 – Adult Programs
Nearly every facility has an adult program with instruction and competition. You can choose from individual or group lessons. As you become more proficient at playing the game, there are many leagues available for social and competitive interaction.

4 – High School Tennis
Many high schools today participate in high school tennis (see chapter Info and Web Pages). There are tryouts for the team and league competition that lead up to state championships. If your son or daughter has some experience playing competition, this is an excellent way to participate with their fellow students in an after-school program that is very cost-effective in getting some more match experience. There are starter kits available for the coaches and players, which can enhance your local school program (see info page).

5 – League Tennis
There are many ways to play competition in tennis, and one of the more enjoyable ones is the leagues or team tennis. In Europe, this is a very important part of tennis tradition. Everyone with a competitive spirit wants to play in the league, may it be beginners or pros. In the United

States, there are many leagues available in every district. Young and old should definitely give it a try!

6 – College Tennis

The United States has a unique situation with college tennis not known to the rest of the world. It is an opportunity to train and play while studying. Most colleges offer great programs with partial or full scholarships for tuition and board. They provide training and competition against other teams and often have their players compete in professional events. (Players cannot accept any prize money due to eligibility of NCAA rules.) It is a great tool in bridging the gap between junior and pro tennis. For others, it is a great opportunity to obtain an education while playing high-level tennis.

Coaching

Finding a coach for the appropriate level of play is important for the development of the player. Teaching beginning players is not only difficult, it also takes great patience and determination to do it right. Starting off with the proper grips, strokes, and footwork is imperative for later improvements. There are coaches for every level of play. You could compare this with teachers at an elementary school level, high school level, or college level. Some coaches are great for beginning players but may not have the skills or experience needed for working with advanced players.

So how do you find the proper coach? First, you have to determine the level of teaching you are looking for and ask around several of the tennis parents and players. You can do some research yourself on the Internet and compare the various programs and their prices. And finally, you can visit some of the practice sessions and talk to the coach. You will be able to communicate your wishes and find out the coaching philosophy and work method of the coach.

A good start saves time and is elemental to any successful result.

DEVELOPING A JUNIOR

There is not one specific way to develop a player, especially considering the many pathways players have taken to reach the top as a junior or a pro. Some have first dominated in the juniors before trying out in pro events. Others have not developed as fast and have gone to college first. In some rare cases, the players have hardly played any junior events and moved to pro events fairly fast. And then there are all the combinations in between. There is not one golden pathway, no standard development that fits all. There are, however, some important steps in your development as a player that can help improve your game. Most of all, try to enjoy the journey!

Building the Foundation

This is all about getting the basics right from the start. You don't want to go back and change strokes or grips and waste time doing it all over again. When starting off playing tennis, your strokes are the blueprint of your game. You will follow this for a good portion of your tennis career. Good and bad habits are formed early on.

A good age to start is around six or seven years of age (or sooner with Quick Start tennis). At this age, the child will have sufficient strength to maneuver and control the racket. This will enhance the chance of developing proper strokes and confidence in the sport. Once the player has learned some basic strokes, it is a good time to begin playing a few matches. A good local program will organize some club matches so the students gradually get used to competition. It takes two to three years for a beginning player to learn enough of the basic strokes and strategies to start competing in 10-and-under, local, or rookie events. Many clubs host these tournaments, and entry fees are minimal.

Finding a good coach to teach the basics (someone who not only has an interest in technique development but who also knows how important it is to keep it fun at the same time). Kids at a young age have a rich imagination and are fond of games. They love to compete against their peers and work in large groups. So finding someone who is experienced in developing juniors and has proven to have good developmental skills with kids is important.

Continuity in coaching is an important factor in the development process. Parents need to consider this factor, especially if they are going to coach their own child. Ask yourself how long you will be able to fulfill this role and if this is the right choice for you and your child. Many players change coaches if they, or their parents, see that other players are more successful with another coach. Especially in tennis, the grass seems to be greener on the other side. Making a change in coaching more often makes you lose time in development and is not really recommended unless it is a necessity. A new coach will often start changing the technique of the player, which often leads to a loss of confidence. Another aspect to consider is that it takes at least a year to master a major change in strokes. The longer a player has been trained to hit the ball a particular way, the longer it takes to change anything. Changes in strokes should only be considered if the current stroke will hamper the player's development and/or they are adamant in making the change themselves.

Playing other sports (cross-training) can have a positive effect on the development of a tennis player. In order for a tennis player to compete at higher levels of play, it is important that they develop an athletic body. This can be done by playing a variety of sports that will not only develop different muscle groups but will also help increase stamina, flexibility coordination, strength, and footwork.

The group size is also a factor to consider at an early stage. It is recommended to have the kids start off in larger groups (groups of four or eight are preferable). This way, they can compare themselves with others. It is good for them to see how other students perform with the same task. Seeing good examples and mistakes is part of the learning process in combination with a healthy dose of competition against different opponents.

Group lessons or private lessons are experienced differently, and participation is dependent on the goals and interest of the player. Don't make it too serious with private lessons early on in their development unless there are some things to correct. After the corrections are made, have them go back to the group. Private lessons at a young age are boring for a child and can hurt the interest in the game. Group lessons give more opportunity to learn from one another. Experiencing good and bad examples from one another promotes students learning at a faster rate.

Academies are very popular these days, and many parents decide to enroll their children every year. If your child is just starting to play the game, these schools are not for you. The academies are much more suited for kids who have had a solid base in stroke development and want to play a lot more tennis. The academies are organized to bring many kids together in a competitive environment to excel through competition. This is an excellent environment for advanced and pro players to improve their tennis game with plenty of practice and match play.

USTA programs are available in every section. They organize many training opportunities from Quick Start, for the novice young players (five to seven years), to training opportunities in the section and match play at the regional training centers. They have three training centers for the top juniors in Los Angeles, New York, and Boca Raton. You are able to call the section office in your section to find out what programs are available for your student (see Info and Web Pages).

Grips and strokes are important at the beginning in learning the game. Bad grips and strokes can be very limiting to improvement in the game since they have a direct result on strategy (see technique training). The level of execution of the strokes will determine how well a player can perform a particular strategy against an opponent. So the start is critical to the development of a player and has long-term effects on the performance. There are a lot of ways to correct these strokes and grips without making it a burden to the child. At an early age, kids don't particularly like technique lessons. So using games as a method to make changes will eventually result in better performance and make it a fun, enjoyable experience for everyone. Imagination and inventiveness, on the part of the coach, is the key!

The proper level of play in tournaments should be adjusted to the motivation and intensity of the player. Playing a level where the student can win some matches helps them gain confidence by finding accomplishment in what they are doing. Not every child wants to be a champion from the beginning. Let them be their own motivator and wait for indications on their level of passion for the game. The student has to be the leader in this. Parents and coaches should not pressure a child to perform at a level they are not ready for. Praise a child for their accomplishments in the match, whether they win or lose. It takes the pressure off to win at all cost in an effort to please the parent. When playing matches, praising a child excessively for winning matches can have side effects and added pressure. This can lead to players acting out on court.

Have a development plan once the player starts taking the game more seriously. The plan will outline how to develop their game from a technical, tactical, mental, and conditional view to fit the style of the player. It will also include training and tournament schedules, when to play, how much to train, and equally as important, when to rest! This plan needs to be made together with the child, coach, and parents. Make it simple and realistic. Be sure it fits your schedule; it is essential to stick to the plan once you have made it. Make sure everyone fully agrees to the plan and has had ample input. Usually, the simple and original plans are the best.

Philosophies of teaching are the principles and teaching method of each individual coach. All coaches need to have a clear vision of what they are expecting to achieve with each player. Whether you are a parent who is trying to coach your own child or you are an experienced coach, it is imperative that you develop a philosophy of coaching and make your direction clear. This will be easier for an experienced coach. In the beginning, a novice coach will not have the experience it takes to fully develop a philosophy of coaching. This is something you will have to develop over time. You can start with a variety of things such as something you are very passionate about or that which made an impression on you as a player. Philosophies often change over time as you gain experience. You may need to try a variety of things to see what works best for you.

Communication is always important in building a good relationship with a player. As a coach, you must communicate not only with your players but also the parents. As a parent, you must communicate with your child, the coach, and the other players and their families. By developing a good relationship with everyone involved, you are helping to promote healthy competition among the players. Communication with a coach should be one of respect. Be supportive and trust their expertise. When you see your child excelling, try to stay calm. Staying down to earth and stimulating your child at the same time is a delicate balance. It is important for children to understand that even if they earn respect for playing tennis well, life does not change in communicating with others and treating everyone with respect.

Andre Agassi

The enjoyment of developing a player is not just in the end result, but the journey it takes us in getting there.

Martin van Daalen

STAGES OF GROWTH AND DEVELOPMENT

It is crucial that parents and coaches understand the growth and development process to know what to expect from children in understanding and performance. Young tennis players all go through several stages of development with various behaviors that are age appropriate. This chapter describes the stages of physical, mental, emotional, and social behaviors at the different age levels to provide a guideline for comprehension and teaching at each age level.

Ages Three to Seven

During the age range from three to seven, children grow relatively fast and learn basic, large motor skills such as running, jumping, crawling, hopping, and skipping, etc. They also learn to throw and catch, skills they use to strike with a bat, paddle, or racket. Children at this age like to play simple physical games that demand very few rules. Coaches and parents need to demonstrate rather than explain the game. The kids are still exploring the world they live in and seeking answers to questions. You can help them by encouragement, asking questions that lead to the answer or setting up situations that require them to experiment. They explore their social skills with their playmates, mostly of the same gender, as they fight over toys, a certain space, or being in charge of a game or such. Coaches and parents should teach the children discipline by setting limits, establishing rules, and bestowing age-appropriate corrections or rewards for behavior.

Tennis instruction should be organized going by the general outline above. Technique instruction is possible but should be kept short and to the basics. The emphasis should be fun! The instruction should be quick and simple in creating a lot of activity. At this age, the Quick Start program and mini-tennis courts work well to introduce the tennis game. As they become more proficient, the kids will easily make the transition to a regular-size tennis court and enjoy it all the more.

Martin van Daalen

Ages Eight to Eleven

During this age period, children grow relatively slow. At the end of this age range, they might, however, show a wide variation in physical maturity. Since girls mature physically faster than boys, most often their coordinative skills will develop quicker. To ensure improvement of the physical developmental skills, it can be very beneficial to expose the kids to different types of sports (cross-training). This all-round approach to physical development will set the groundwork to specializing later on, if desired. Kids this age seem to have endless energy in playing and learning. They look up to adults to provide them with all the answers to their questions. They will start to adhere to the rules and seek the approval of others. Their self-worth and confidence will develop through positive experiences and by accomplishing tasks. Their social development is influenced by their family values, their socioeconomic stature, and their ability of independency.

During these years, the growth of the skeletal structure is still in development. To avoid serious injuries, strength training should only be performed using their own body weight. Flexibility training can help improve strength and prevent problems with joint movement at a later stage.

The tennis instruction can be tennis specific but should be explained using the game approach. Teaching kids how to play the game tactically by executing the strokes technically will make more sense to them. This age-group is critical in developing the fundamental skills for a solid foundation of the game. Practice and repetition of the different strokes are required to build patterns of play and are beneficial to gaining confidence in playing the game.

Ages Twelve to Fifteen

The most important physical and mental change in a child's life is the puberty phase. It can start as early as ten years or as late as eighteen years of age. Female tennis players tend to reach puberty a little earlier at an average of about thirteen years of age. With boys, this is usually around the age of fifteen. Coaches and parents need to be aware that females may struggle with body image issues that can lead to eating disorders and emotional instability.

The physical growth is fastest during the first two years of puberty, with the girls starting approximately two years ahead of the boys. On average, girls reach full adult height at sixteen while boys reach it at nineteen. Mental development now exhibits formal thoughts and logical operations. They can start to grasp abstract ideas, and there is some progression in moral reasoning. The social development is strongly influenced by peer pressure. They have their own culture, and they are constantly trying new roles.

Coaches and parents need to be patient during this age-group. Tennis might not be the most important thing in their lives. With the wide range of physical and mental development in this age-group, success in tennis can vary widely due to early and late developers. The skills learned at an early age need to be reinforced during this period as the style will mostly carry on for a lifetime. Players must experiment different styles and will need some assistance in choosing the correct one that works best for them.

Ages Sixteen to Eighteen

With girls maturing at a younger age, they could reach their plateau of improvement early and become discouraged with their progress. It is not uncommon to see girls lose interest at this stage whereas boys are just reaching their potential. Physical growth can vary at this stage, with late developers catching up with early developers.

Teenagers can show a tremendous effort toward a goal in showing how much they want to achieve. At the same time, they might abuse their bodies with lack of sleep, a poor diet, and illegal substances. Even though they are capable of advanced reasoning, they often believe their behavior will have no ill effect on their game. They will often question authority, history, and tradition in order the find a sense of self-worth. The social pressures are still very strong at this time as independent thinking starts to develop among some of the adolescents. Parents and coaches must reinforce this independence if they want to assist in the transition to adulthood. Decisions about college start to emerge as kids are faced with choices on different schools, driving, dating, drugs, and maybe a part-time job. Parents need to be involved, interested, and supportive without making all the decisions. Listening alone can be of great help. The tennis development depends for a great deal on what has occurred at earlier ages. For gifted and talented players, it is the time to make serious life choices about training and competition. In exceptional cases, this means making choices about a professional career and postponing college. However, for most, it means development of their game to compete in high school and college. Players need to adopt a style and master the patterns of play. The competitive skills also need to be enhanced in learning to cope with pressure during matches, the weather, environment, difficult opponents, and unexpected situations. These are all valuable experiences in tennis and in life.

Basic Rules in Teaching Young Juniors

1. **Children should not be treated as young adults.** Even though kids might react the same as adults at time, you still need to take their age and their physical and mental development into consideration. Parents and coaches need to be encouraging the players without forcing them into adult expectations.

2. **Know the growth and development of each age-group.** By understanding the growth and development of each individual player, parents and coaches can adjust the approach in raising a child and training to appropriate levels of expectations. Knowledge of the developmental stages can be of great influence in teaching proper behaviors and attitudes.

3. **Individualize the training to the growth and development of each child.** Even though kids might be the same age, it does not mean each player will develop at the same rate. Though all children reach milestones within a specific time frame, each individual child has their own rate of growth and development. Experienced coaches will know how much they can demand from a child on a physical and mental level.

4. **Show proper examples of behavior and attitude at all times.** Children look up to adults for the examples in life. They often copy adults in how they act, what they say, and how they behave. So be very careful to always show proper behavior and attitudes at all times.

The differences in growth and development is what makes us all unique as individuals and as tennis players.

Steffi Graf

METHODOLOGY OF TEACHING

What is the methodology of teaching?

- *An organized system to teaching*
- *A study of organized systems and principles to teaching*

In other words, this means that you use a systematic approach to teaching tennis in a simple but logical order.

For example, you would not start teaching a topspin forehand or a topspin service to a beginning junior. Without a good order of teaching, players will get easily frustrated since the topics are not within their grasp of experience and racket control. By trying to hit shots they are not able to master yet, they will also become very inconsistent and haphazard in their ability to play the game.

A couple of ground rules to the methodology of teaching:

1. **Systematic approach**: *Go from A to B to C, meaning that you start teaching at the beginning and do not skip steps to get to the final goal.*

2. **Logical competency order**: *Go from easy to more complicated topics. Learn the basics first and maintain a simple approach with each next step in the learning process.*

3. **Master the skill**: *Don't move on to the next skill level or subject until the student has mastered it to a certain degree of excellence and confidence.*

4. **Repeat the practice:** *Keep repeating the practice to maintain the skill level of the stroke or subject.*

In following these simple rules of teaching, your student will have a much better understanding in learning the game. In addition, they will master it more rapidly, hold up under pressure, and play with more confidence.

Determine What You Want or Need to Teach

- A new subject in the progression of learning
- A correction to an error in learning

A *new subject progression* means finding the right order of exercises and drills for a new subject to make the learning process as smooth as possible.

A *correction to an error in learning* is more complicated. There are several steps you have to follow to ensure that what you are about to teach is going to remedy the error.

The steps to follow in making corrections:

1. **Analysis**
2. **Error detection**
3. **Correction**
4. **Post analysis**

You start by making an ***analysis*** of the overall subject to correct. This, to narrow down the area in which to look for the error and to make sure it is not caused by some other factor.

Error detection is the crucial part of the correction. Making an initial mistake in error detection will lead to more complication in corrections.
Corrections need to be handled with a progression in learning that stimulates the learning process. Give explanation as to what you are about to change and why. Furthermore, explain how you want to go about making these changes. This process will facilitate confidence in your corrections.

The ***post analysis*** is the analysis after the correction has been made. This is done to make sure that the correction was the right one and that the error has been corrected properly.

A method of teaching will promote a purpose to training.

Anna Kournikova

THE BASICS OF TEACHING

Basic Strokes

There are some basic strokes the player must learn in order to play the game. These vary according to the age of the player and their competency level.

In learning the game of tennis, there are four basic strokes. When starting the game, keep it simple with just the first three. When the player shows more consistency in how and when to use these, you can add the volley to their repertoire of strokes. All four basic strokes have to work in unison with one another in order to be effective in playing the game.

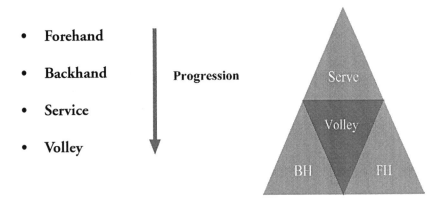

- **Forehand**

- **Backhand**   **Progression**

- **Service**

- **Volley**

The Four Pillars of Tennis

In teaching the game it takes more than just teaching the strokes. The game consists of four major teaching aspects that form the pillars of the game. These teaching and learning aspects are:

- *Technical*
  Learning the mechanics of the strokes in order to execute them with consistent repetition for practice and match play

- *Tactical*
  Learning how to use the strokes in developing patterns of play to outmaneuver your opponent or to take advantage of their weaknesses

- *Mental*
  Learning how to control the emotions and thoughts during practice and match play in order to control the execution

- *Physical*
  Learning how to use the available physical ability to maximize the advantage in practice and match play

Subjects of Teaching

When teaching subjects, there is a logical order and method in how to introduce them to your students. Whenever you are teaching, always keep in mind the technical, tactical, physical, and mental implications. We call these the four pillars of the game. It is important that you and your students understand the concept of how the four pillars of the game are connected and how they work together. An example would be when teaching the service action; when teaching a technical aspect, you should also explain what the tactical purpose is, what the physical aspects and mental implications are, and how to use these aspects in match situations.

Teaching Order (easy to difficult)

1. Consistency   (for rookie players
2. Depth   and beginners these
3. Change of direction   three subjects only)

4. Spin   (these subjects are for
5. Power   advanced players and
6. Tempo   tournament players)

(In teaching and training in this first book and the level we are working with, only the first three aspects are of importance for now.)

Consistency is the first requirement in anything you teach in tennis. The execution of the technique, in combination with good footwork, is the key to obtaining more consistency. Consistency is imperative to be successful at any level of play in tennis.

Examples of poor consistency: Not watching the ball properly will result in off-center hits. Not hitting the ball at the proper contact point, out in front of the body, will result in poor direction. Not getting in position early enough will result in mistakes. Not using the knees and getting "under" the ball will result in hitting the ball in the net.

Note: Make sure your students are aware how to improve consistency in whatever subject they are practicing or using in point play. Do not move on to the next subject until there is proficiency acquired and a comfort level with the subject is obtained.

Training: - Make goals in hitting the ball as often as possible.
- Make a game that involves consistency!
- Use consistency different ways: the stroke, a pattern, or strategy.

Consistency is fundamental to any successful tennis player.

Depth to strokes is most easily obtained with the trajectory chosen over the net. The combination of speed and height of the ball over the net determines the depth of the ball in the court. Depth is important at all levels of play and even more so with advanced and professional players. With more depth on the shots, it is more difficult for the opponent to create an angle and the player has more time to react to shots due to the length of the trajectory.

Example 1: When hitting the ball close to the baseline, the opponent is forced to move back. The depth of the stroke might catch the opponent on the back foot and result in a less powerful stroke and a shorter return of the ball. The player is able to attack the short ball and finish the point at the net.

Example 2: When retrieving an angle shot from the opponent, the length of the returning trajectory provides more reaction time to recover to the middle of the court. Depth is a key factor in playing neutralizing and defensive shots.

Note: Make sure your students are well aware on how to create depth with the use of the trajectory of the ball (speed and height). Make sure your students understand the tactical advantages to play with depth.

Training: - *An easy way to train depth to the ball is with the use of targets or a marked-off area to hit within.*
- *Use the net stick under the middle of the net to make players hit higher over the net. With the same speed, more height results in more depth.*

Change of direction is the skill of moving the ball to one or different targets on the court in order to make the opponent move and to force a mistake. The angle of the oncoming ball, the position of the player on the court, and the chosen target are all factors in changing direction. To obtain proficiency in changing direction with consistency and depth takes much practice and patience at any level of play.

Note: Make sure your students understand the importance of early preparation, footwork, and contact points in making direction and the change of direction.

Training: - *Playing to one specific target is a great way to practice the precision of strokes.*
- *Changing direction trains the timing and precision to different targets.*
- *You can make a combination of these two by having one player hit to one side of the court and the other alternate shots to both sides of the court.*

Roger Federer

THE LEARNING PROCESS

There are many ways to teach tennis. An experienced coach will use several different methods to keep his students interested, focused, and physically challenged. Knowing different approaches of teaching can be very helpful whenever the student is not responding to one specific training method. Players learn by the information provided to them and the way they receive this information. Keep in mind that many players learn a different way or a combination of the following:

Auditory - Hearing (listening to an explanation and description of the subject)

Visually - Seeing (seeing an example or demonstration of the subject)

Sensory - Feeling (feeling the action or motion performed)

Intuitive - Instinct (a natural instinct how to perform the action or situation)

Players might respond to one of these senses of learning alone or a combination of two or more. Every student is different in that respect; and it is important, as a coach, to understand how your student learns best. Here are some different teaching methods to use:

- *Teaching auditory*
  The actual teaching is the explaining of what to do and how. Explaining in detail what to train and why, how the execution should be, and how long to perform the exercise.

- *Demonstrating*
  The demonstration will indicate exactly how to perform the action by showing a proper example. You can perform this yourself, but it can be very beneficial to have it performed by others to make sure everyone understands.

- *Manually directing*
  This is a teaching method where you physically touch the racket, the person, or both together to guide them through the proper action.

- *Visualizing*
  This method requires thinking about the motion or action as if watching a film. Closing your eyes helps you focus with seeing the action in your thoughts.

- *Giving assignments*
  Giving assignments will help the students coach themselves once they are on the court playing a match. This method trains them to get used to task solving. You can do this either with a closed end (the drill stops at the end of the task) or open end (playing out the point once the task is performed).

- *Initiating discussion*
  The discussion should be with a question-and-answer session that should be a two-way conversation between the coach and the student.

Different Ways of Teaching

There are several different methods to use when teaching players. Each method has a philosophy in approach and execution, and teaching them requires some practice. Players respond differently to each training method. It is up to the coach to find out what speaks to the player the most.

- **The Rhythm Method**
  This method of teaching uses the rhythm of the stroke and the timing of the bounce of the ball with the contact point. The coach uses this method to stimulate timing in order to improve technique and consistency. This method is also very useful in creating smooth and relaxed strokes to improve fluidity and efficiency. **An example**: Use counting out loud to assist with the rhythm of the bounce of the ball and impact with the ball.

Martin van Daalen

- **The Balance Method**

  The balance of the body before, during, and after the stroke will influence the execution of the stroke. The balance method of teaching uses these three balance points in the swing to stabilize the stroke and improve consistency in performance. This can be performed with and without the recovery footwork as long as speed and tempo are adjusted. **An example**: Hold the position after the stroke is performed to see if balance can be maintained. This method improves the preparation of the strokes, the overall balance, and the recovery of the strokes.

- **The Contact Point Method**

  The contact points of the strokes are the largest determining factor of the trajectory and direction. The contact method is fundamental in showing the mechanics of the stroke and is a reference point in the key positions (see technical training). Using the contact method can help improve the timing of the strokes and positively improve the technical execution and consistency in performance. **An example**: Blocking the ball at contact before playing it back over the net will enhance the contact point and make players very aware of the impact area. The player can also call out a word at the time of contact to improve the timing of the contact point. *Note: Many top players use this method with their breathing by exhaling at the moment of contact. You might have noticed this more clearly when listening to some of the girls on tour.*

- **The Combination Method**

  This method of teaching uses a combination of two or all three of the methods to improve the strokes. A combination of these methods can greatly improve certain strokes or a certain aspect of the stroke in order to improve the whole action. If a player does not respond as well to one method, you can try another method or a combination of methods. Being flexible in teaching different methods to suit your student will improve the learning process and cut down the learning time.

ORGANIZING YOUR TEACHING

In becoming a tennis coach, you have to make a decision on what philosophy and style of coaching you are going to adopt. This will help you determine your method of teaching and how you want to structure your lessons. There are also many different types of coaches, and you have to choose the one you aspire to be. It could be that you intend to be a club pro or work as a college coach. Your goal could be to develop top juniors or coach professionals, work at an academy, or even start up your own program. Whatever it may be, make sure you have a strategy in developing your coaching career. In the chart below, you can see an example of how the process of you teaching should evolve:

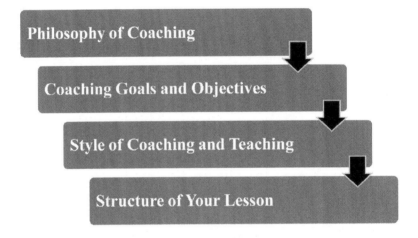

The **philosophy of coaching** has to be your own individual viewpoints, values, and beliefs on how to teach and coach tennis players with a certain method and style.

The **coaching goals and objectives** are determined by your own vision of your aspirations and ambitions as a coach and teacher.

Martin van Daalen

The **style of coaching** is an adaption of your teaching and coaching that fits your character and personality and transcends in your communication with the students.

The **structure of your lesson** is the organization, format, and execution of the material you aim use in teaching your lesson.

When you are organizing your teaching, you have to think about all these factors so your students and their parents (and possible employer) receive a clear picture of what your expectations are as a coach.

Programs

There are several ways of organizing programs for your students. This will largely depend on the different work situations and facilities you use for coaching. The programs you can offer are as follows:

1. Group lessons
2. Private lessons
3. League training
4. Junior development program
5. Adult programs
6. Academy-style training program
7. Coaching at tournaments

By providing some explanation on each of the programs and the cost involved, you will be perceived as organized and professional. All these programs have to be coordinated with the facility where you teach due to court availability and the number of students.

Scheduling

The organization of your hours during the day should be coordinated to the type of programs and your other possible duties as a coach. These responsibilities could vary from meetings with other coaches to discuss student programs and scheduling to maintenance or administrative duties. Below is an example of a daily schedule:

Time	Duties
8:00-8:30	Meeting about students and program
8:30-9:00	Lesson planning for the day
9:00-12:00	Teaching adults and/or league training
12:00-1:00	Lunch
1:00-3:00	Private instruction
3:00-6:00	Group lessons or academy training
6:00-6:30	Administrative duties

As you can see in the schedule above, you should organize your time to make a plan for each group or private lesson and write some notes at the end of the day about the progress and corrections of your students.

It is better to schedule adults in the morning as they usually have more flexibility in their daily schedule. Most kids are in school during the day and will only have time in the afternoon.

Lesson Plan

The organization of a lesson plan is an important factor to the development plan you have set out for your students. Otherwise, it is very easy to stray from your goals and intentions and end up just hitting balls without a purpose. Preferably, you want to have a purpose every time you step on the court to get the most out of every lesson. When thinking about making your lesson plan, you should consider the following:

- **Number of Students**
  The number of students for each lesson can vary. To make a good lesson plan, you need to know how many students are participating. This will assist you in booking the right number of courts. The number of students can influence the topic you are intending for your lesson or a different way of introducing the material. Are the students going to play with each other, or are you going to feed the balls to them? This could result in needing assistance of one or more coaches.

Martin van Daalen

- **Level of Play**
The level of play is of great importance in choosing the proper subjects. The lesson content needs to be appropriate to the skill level of the players. If it is too difficult for them to perform, they will become frustrated and maybe discouraged. If the material is too easy, they will become bored and lose interest very quickly. The level of play is also important in pairing players together with the same skill level. This helps you, as a coach, to make your lessons run smoothly, and it allows the players to compete against one another.

- **Surface**
There are three types of surfaces that are very common to players and coaches alike: hard courts, clay courts, and carpet (indoor). When organizing your lesson, take in consideration the surface you are training on. Coordinating the practice content with the surface can assist you in their performance and confidence. The footwork and strokes can also be specific to a particular type of surface. The practice of certain styles of play is also specific to the surface.

- **Weather**
The weather condition will, many times, have an effect on the performance of the players. With extreme heat or cold, you have to take precautions to provide sufficient breaks. Water needs to be readily available at all times. Note: In windy and colder conditions, your students can become more dehydrated than you would anticipate. Adjusting the lesson content to the weather conditions can be very helpful in teaching your students how to deal with these conditions.

- **Equipment**
The use of specialized equipment in training can enhance the performance of your students. For instance, they can be used to help visualize a target area or barrier. There are many companies available to purchase these online. Be prepared in organizing the equipment ahead of time for your lessons.

- **Safety**
The safety of the students should always be a primary concern when you are practicing drills or playing matches. The practice area should always be kept free of balls or equipment that could cause your students

trip. Make sure your drills or exercises stay within the limits of the practice area so your students don't run into the fence or net post.

Lesson Types

Group Lessons

Group lessons are a great place to start playing tennis. They are organized so that all players involved are at a similar-skill level. This creates a competitive environment in which students often excel more rapidly. In this setting, players can learn from other players. It is also less expensive than private lessons. It is important to give the player time to develop basic skills before isolating them and starting too soon with private instruction. *Academy-style training* is the same format as group lessons, but it is organized several times a week. This style of coaching can be beneficial if the student is passionate about the game and wants to train more often. *Note: prices are usually lower for group lessons, depending on the group size, skill level, and time of instruction.*

Private Lessons

For novice players, private lessons work best in conjunction with group instruction. This allows them to maintain contact with their peers while providing them an additional opportunity to excel. A good time to consider private lessons is when a player is showing passion for the sport that goes beyond a recreational level. The general cost for private instruction can be around thirty to fifty dollars but can also range much higher when working with an experienced or veteran coach.

Match Play

Match play can be organized several ways. First, you have to determine your goal in practicing match play, then determine the number of students involved and if you will be practicing singles or doubles matches. This will affect the number of courts needed.

During match play instruction, give your student the opportunity to self-coach by giving them one or two subjects to practice during the competition. Examples would be giving them a strategy or tactic to execute or the performance of a stroke or pattern. Having match play sessions with your students can be very beneficial in allowing the students to apply what they have learned. It is important that they receive coaching and feedback in the process.

Visual Training Lessons

The viewing of matches, training or video can be very inspiring and beneficial to the learning process (especially to the students with visual learning abilities). These lessons are an excellent substitution on a rainy day and a valuable asset to your teaching.

Lesson Plan   (1 hour)

1. **Warm-up**	10 min	
2. **Technical part**	20 min	Part A
3. **Tactical/mental/physical**	15 min	Part B
4. **Point play**	10 min	Part C
5. **Recap of the lesson**	5 min	

This is the basic format for a lesson plan. Part A is the main topic, part B, and part C are the application part of the main subject. In this lesson plan, the technical aspect of the game is the main subject. Tactical/mental/physical (part B) and point play (part C) are the application part of the main subject. You can change which of these is the main topic, but you must be sure to include A, B, and C in order for your students to learn how important each part is and how they all fit together.

Warm-Up

The purpose of the warm-up is to physically and mentally prepare players for the workout. It is not only to loosen up and stretch the muscles but also to provide the students with a heightened sense of awareness for better performance. A good warm-up consists of some running with specific footwork exercises that are geared toward tennis (hops, skips, side steps, lunges, etc.) Some dynamic stretching and static stretching is important as well to prevent injuries during training. (With very young kids, the warm-up works best by using some sort of game with movement.)

Technical Part

This section of the lesson is most often the main topic. It should reflect the subject from the training plan that is scheduled for this day or week. The subject matter should be a new topic or the next sequence in the learning process that represents a logical order (methodology). When teaching this section, try to explain the topic with precise and simple concepts so they can immediately get to work on the execution of the exercise. Try to keep the intensity high by giving them sufficient short breaks. Note: In teaching the technical subjects, keep in mind that you can substitute a tactical subject in this part A. Sometimes it makes it easier to explain the stroke production by showing how it is used in a point or match (tactical).

Tactical, Mental, Physical Part
This section should represent the application of part A. After learning the subject matter in part A, you want to be sure the students comprehend how to use it in a match play. This can be done by practicing patterns or points.

Note: This section of the learning process is usually totally forgotten or left out. Most coaches spend 95 percent of the time only on technique, with very little time on tactical or mental development. Don't forget that even with beginning players, the reason they play the game is to compete against their peers. The more you can help them achieve better results in doing so, the more they will appreciate your training. Teaching them all aspects of the game helps them to become a well-rounded player.

Point Play
Playing points is an important part of group lessons. Young kids love the competition. Make it fun and entertaining for all and mix up the games with a wide variety of activities. Rotating the opponents at the beginner level, regardless of strength, gives everyone a chance to learn from each other.

Recap
The recap should be used to suggest some topics to practice on their own during the week. This is also a great time to make announcements about the next lesson time, the upcoming tournaments, entry dates, etc.

Martin van Daalen

Andy Roddick

Lesson Plan (example)

Name: Player A
Date:
Time:

Warm-up: - Run around the court
- Skips, side steps, lunges, etc.
- Stretching

Part A (teaching part):
Service action
- Teaching the toss (accuracy)
- Teaching racket motion (grip)
- Teaching combination

Part B (application part):
Service targets
- Forehand side of service box
- Backhand side of service box
- Practice different targets

Part C (point play): - Play points including the service action
- Play points, serving to backhand

Recap: - Toss accuracy for better technique
- Service accuracy for tactical advantage

Martin van Daalen

Pete Sampras as a junior

TECHNICAL INSTRUCTION

This part of the instruction is the mechanics of the stroke you want to present. The mechanics of the stroke can either be taught as a whole or in parts. The instruction should be short, comprehensive, and a part of a progression. To reinforce the instruction, you want to get the students on the court so they can apply the lesson immediately

Here are some guidelines for technical instructions:

- **Explain Why This Topic or Change**
  The explanation should be concise and as short as possible to avoid any misunderstanding about the topic of training. Ask the students if they have any questions before they start the exercise.

- **Introduce the Whole-Part-Whole Method**
  Sometimes, it works easier to break down the action in parts and then, at the end, put the whole action back together again. The service action is a good example as this works well with small kids and novice tennis players. With detecting errors in the strokes, you can put the focus on a certain part (key position) of the stroke. Example: backswing, contact point, or follow through.

- **Slow Things Down**
  Most kids like to hit the ball as hard as they can. Slowing the action down allows the students to feel what is actually going on with the strokes. It will also help ensure they are learning to use the proper technique.

- **Impart Less Power for Better Coordination**
  When using too much power, you will experience less coordination and timing. There have been several studies to determine the maximum amount of power and the tipping point at what point the coordination decreases. This point is a proximally at 60 percent of your maximum power (see graph next page). As you can see, the curve (coordination level) starts to decrease around 60 percent. This is also the case with

Martin van Daalen

long matches over time. Toward the end of those matches, more power (energy) is required for the same action.

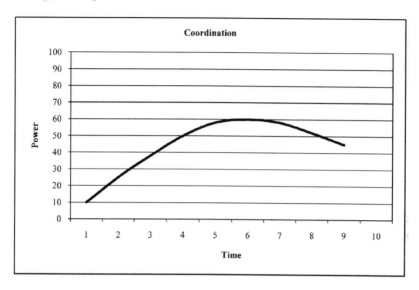

Note: A good method to detect if your student is using too much power is to ask how much grip pressure they are using while hitting the ball. You can suggest a range from 1 to 10, with 10 being the highest. Grip pressure should be around 5 or 6, but some top players have even less grip pressure.

A method to reduce grip pressure during practice is to have the players show their fingers at the follow through of the stroke. The players will notice an increase of touch with the strokes and an increase of timing and coordination. Most often, the speed of the ball will increase as well with the added flexibility and the elasticity of the elbow and wrist by relaxing the hand.

- **Provide Repetition**
  Lots of repetition is needed to master the strokes and patterns on the tennis court. It is wise to continually repeat the drills and training so that, eventually, it becomes an automated motion or action

- **Don't Skip Steps**
  Moving too fast with the development program of your players can be detrimental. It is possible you will skip steps to achieve your goals quicker. There is a good chance that the student will get confused

with too much information before they have a chance to master the subjects first. Another possibility is that the students won't retain the information very long with less practice time. The new subjects will soon follow one another to quickly and move beyond their skill level.

- **Provide Encouragement**
  Praising the student is important for their confidence and their performance. Too much praise can be harmful with the student becoming overconfident and not trying as hard. Too little praise will make them very critical of themselves and very frustrated. A good balance is required to stimulate them with a realistic view on how to keep pushing themselves to excel.

- **Get Feedback from Students**
  Asking questions to your students and receiving feedback on how they experience the training is important. You might get some input to improve your next training. Finding out what works and what doesn't can be very helpful to your development plan and how to proceed from that point on.

Mistakes and Errors

There is a difference between mistakes and errors. Mistakes are well-executed strokes that are hit with the best intentions but still go in the net or out of the court. Errors are lapses in judgment with incorrect shot choices. For instance, returning the ball flat and low over the net out of a defensive position instead of higher over the net with some topspin would be considered an error. Mistakes are mostly from a technical or physical origin whereas errors are mostly from a tactical or mental origin. Just remember that even the best players make mistakes. Understanding the difference and making the right decisions is important for both the player and the coach. Giving the wrong corrections to mistakes can be detrimental to the player.

Directions and Corrections

This is the most important part of the actual teaching with the most impact on the development of the student. Those first impressions are imprinted in the student's memory. So you can imagine how important the message and delivery are at this time.

This part of the instruction is where I see new coaches make the most mistakes! Often, the coach or parent does not have enough experience and/or has no training as a coach. Just try to imagine how you would feel, as a patient, to receive a diagnosis from an unlicensed doctor. There is no shortcut to experience, so train yourself well and become an experienced coach first before providing instruction. Coaches should stay emotionally removed from the outcome of the match. As a parent coach, you might let your emotions control your instruction. Unlike parents, being emotionally detached from the player makes it easier for coaches to give sound advice for their development. My recommendations would be as follows:

1. Hire an experienced coach whenever possible.
2. As a parent, train yourself as a coach before giving instruction.
3. To become a good coach, stay emotionally detached from results

- **Make Corrections Immediately**
  When improper strokes or bad habits persist too long, they become ingrained in the muscle memory of the student. It takes less time to train the student correctly than to undo those errors! This is definitely the case with novice players, but it can also happen with more advanced players. Make sure to find the proper time to make the corrections. If the player is really frustrated, they will be less receptive. Find a moment when the player has calmed down with a break in the action before assisting the player. When players have already received corrections earlier, wait to see if they remember the information first before making corrections again. If they still don't remember, ask a question to make them think without providing the answer right away. When they are able to remember the correction, it will stick with them much longer than if you provide it for them all the time. You, as a coach, should help them in training their own memory.

- **Correct One Thing at a Time**
  Providing too much information at one time is confusing for the student. With just one thing to think about, they will have a much easier learning process. Ideally, you want this learning process as a tool

to (1) learn the correction, (2) give them plenty of time to practice, (3) try it in points and matches, and (4) master it before moving on.

- **Correct the Main Mistake First**
  When making corrections, it is important to find the origin of the mistake. This takes experience and a keen eye. Detecting the root of the problem is critical before trying to solve all the side effects. Sometimes, it can be very obvious, but it can also be hidden and not visible to the naked eye. It might require slow-motion video to detect any faults. For example, to detect defects in strokes follow this method:

  1. look at contact point of the stroke (the grip can be of influence).
  2. look at the key positions of the stroke (see chapters on key positions).
  3. look at the balance of the body (before, during and after the stroke).

- **Make a Positive Remark before Correcting**
  The student's state of mind is of importance at the time of a correction. Students can be very sensitive and may take corrections personally or feel you are insulting their performance. Female players are often more emotional than males. No matter what gender you are coaching, positive reinforcement is the key to successful corrections. There are several ways to achieve positive communication with your student. The first method is to wait for the proper execution and to immediately remark on how well that was performed. The second method is to remark on a positive improvement from another subject before introducing the correction. The third method is to start a conversation and ask a question on how to improve the subject.

- **Don't Move on till It Is Mastered**
  Mastering the game of tennis takes time and patience. Be sure your players have conquered the skill you are teaching before moving on to the next subject. Give players ample time to practice and implement your instructions

- **When Corrections Don't Work, Use Another Method**
  Not everyone reacts to directions the same way. Some players are visually inclined and like to see video or an example shown to them.

Others are auditory or sensory inclined and you have to explain things or let them feel the sensation of the action. Knowing how your player absorbs information can be very helpful in speeding up the learning process. And even then, you might have to try different methods if one does not appeal to him or her.

In becoming a good coach, you have to learn to be flexible and find what works for them, not just what works for you!

- **Keep Your Voice and Demeanor in Check**
  Your voice and body language sends a message to the player. The playing style and body language of a player sends a message to their opponent! The difference in coaching lies not only in what you say and do but also how you deliver the message. You want to be calm and determined in your delivery just as you would expect to be in a match. Your voice and body language will often show your emotions. Especially if you are coaching as a parent! So be aware and keep your emotions under control.

- **The Best Corrections Are Indirect or Subconscious Corrections**
  Students become very nervous and uptight when they are overly aware of what to improve. They can become so focused on the correction that they tense up and become frustrated. To introduce the topic in an indirect or subconscious way can be very helpful. For example, if players have trouble following through with the forehand, make them catch the racket above the other shoulder with the other hand. By focusing on catching the racket, they will loosen up the hitting arm automatically and follow through much more smoothly. There are many more indirect coaching methods like this that have a positive impact on another subject of improvement. Here are some examples:

1. To improve the follow through and depth on the baseline strokes, have the players imagine they are hitting through a window hanging above the net. This visualization of a target area above the net will accomplish faster results through indirect corrections.

2. To improve better contact points and cleaner shot production, write big numbers on a few balls. The players call them out just

before they make contact. They will be able to read the number just before contact and improve the focus on the ball.

3. To improve touch and fluidity of the strokes, the players must release and show the fingers at the end of the follow through. The release of the fingers will reduce the grip pressure and increase coordination and acceleration of the follow through.

4. To improve the hip and shoulder turn of the stroke, train the players to pose at the end of the stroke with the back foot on the tip of the toe. The players will be thinking of the follow through instead of the turn of the hip and shoulders. The coordination of the hip and shoulder turn will occur with a smooth rotation.

5. To improve acceleration and release of the service action, the player has to focus on the throwing action of a ball. By throwing a ball and then making the connection with the service action, the player will think of the throwing action instead of the separate mechanics of the service action

MOST COMMON MISTAKES WITH INSTRUCTION

Not having a plan can cause all sorts of problems in the development of a player. To practice without a plan is a waste of your time and the student's time. Inevitably, you will forget a topic or you will not follow a logical or proper progression of teaching. A plan will ensure efficiency of learning with the most chance of progress and development to instill a higher level of confidence

Not following a progression of learning is the most common mistake made in teaching and instructions. It usually stems from not formulating a plan first and following a sequence of learning from easy to more complex. I have seen many local pros teach by starting at the end of the sequence without providing the player time to experience all the different steps in between and gradually gain confidence over time. Players have difficulty learning without confidence to support them and will not sustain it very long

Not teaching the proper topics for the level of play is detrimental to the progress of beginners and intermediate players. Even though they might initially be intrigued by the new topics, if they are not appropriate for their level of play, it will undermine their progress and discipline in executing basic fundamentals of the technique. Eventually, they will become frustrated and disappointed with their progress and lose confidence

Having your student hit too hard is not helping you or the student in mastering the strokes or a skill. Hitting the ball hard is associated with top players and playing better tennis. The opposite is the case in developing beginners and intermediate players. The control of the ball and proper execution of the strokes should always be the most important focus in your teaching and coaching. The other problem arises when coaches themselves hit too hard with their students. The players need to be challenged without your ego getting in the way of their progress. By playing consistently above their level of play, they will pick up bad habits and become sloppy in the execution of the strokes. By increasing the speed and tempo occasionally, you will challenge them without causing permanent damage to the technique and discouraging them.

Not stressing the basic fundamentals and grips will create sloppy players without consistency of strokes and lack of confidence during play. The fundamentals of the strokes will give the players points of recognition during the swing (key positions). It will eventually create an automation of the swing through repetition and practice. The grips can be adjusted to the situation and the shot choice but still need to be consistent to execute the stroke with confidence. Coaches that pay less attention to detail will develop players with limitations to their game and development as a player.

Giving corrections without making an analysis will often cause the coach to make the wrong correction. A wrong correction could cause one or more complications in executing the stroke. Making a proper analysis first is the key to good instructions. The coach should check the grips and key positions of the motion to find possible errors in the stroke production instead of acting impulsively without caution. Not everyone has a talented eye to analyze strokes, but with a proper method, you can train yourself.

Giving the wrong cues with corrections causes misunderstanding and confusion. Cues are short instructions, sentences, or key words that indicate a certain action. If these are instructed incorrectly, they will give the wrong impression of the action. This is where the education of the coach plays an important role not only to learn the basic fundamentals but also how to instruct them. A few examples of wrong cues:

"Stay down on the stroke"—This is a much-used cue by coaches and gives students the wrong idea of what actually should happen. Players have to extend out of the knees while hitting the ball to produce power from the ground up and to push forward against the ball. You just don't want players to do this too soon or jump too much while doing it. The timing of the knees is the key. The *correct cue* "Time your knees to extend during contact" *Explanation:* Bend your knees to load the muscles and prepare for the stroke and extend your knees while making contact with the ball. Push upward while keeping the weight of your body against the ball.

"Take the racket back early"—This is a phrase you hear frequently from coaches, and it can actually cause a lot of problems. The backswing needs be to be halfway back instead of all the way back so that the player can use gravity on the arm and racket to initiate power to the forward swing. Taking the backswing back too early will also deteriorate the coordination, timing, and rhythm of the swing. The *correct cue* "Time the backswing with the speed of the ball" *Explanation:* Calmly prepare the forward swing with a ready position at the top of the backswing. Execute the forward swing by dropping the racket from the top in the strike zone of the ball in front of the body.

"Watch the ball"—There is rarely a problem of students not watching the ball. They might not watch it all the way till contact because they are not timing the ball out in front. Watching the trajectory and judging the bounce and spin of the ball to take up position in the right spot is usually the problem. Most beginning players do not rotate the shoulders forward toward contact and end up hitting the ball at the side of the body instead of in front. This makes the tracking of the eyes with the trajectory of the ball very complicated, especially in the final approach to contact. So be careful with the cue: "Watch the ball" Most often, it will be something entirely different. The *correct cue* "Watch the ball until you can see it make contact through the strings" *Explanation:* By tracking the trajectory of the ball, it will be easier to time the contact point with the ball. By watching the ball make contact with the strings behind the racket, you are ensured to hit the ball out in front of the body

Making the correct cues at the correct time in the development of a player is the key to the progress of a player. The cues have to fit in the technical, physical, tactical, and mental development of a player and the progression of the practice. The cues need to be precise and to the point to make an impact on the player. The cues have to be easy to understand and contain no double meaning to eliminate any misunderstanding.

Underestimating the importance of footwork is common with many players and coaches. Tennis is a movement and positioning sport. Good strokes do not help you if the ball is out of your reach. Strokes and footwork are dependent on each other in order to play the game with success. Coaches need to teach players the art of tennis specific movements, positioning, and recovering. Without these attributes, they will never reach their potential.

All practice and no play is a sure way to kill the spirit and passion for the game. As a coach, it is important to understand the stages of development of each student without forgetting why they play the game—to have fun!

Coaches should use a games approach to teaching and instill the competitive spirit while teaching the fundamentals of the game. It does not have to be all games or just all teaching. A good coach will make his students want to practice to play the game with more success. That is why teaching has to involve a learning part, a practice part, and an application part. You can stimulate your students to practice harder by adding a competitive component to the practice and by making it fun

Martin van Daalen

GRIPS

There are many ways to hit the ball in tennis. These different strokes demand a variety of grips. When starting to play tennis, the use of the proper grips speeds up the learning process. Proper grips stimulate better stroke production and the efficiency of motion. It is comparable with the foundation of a house. If the foundation of the house is strong and sturdy, the house will stand for a long time. The same goes for grips. Starting with the right grips is fundamental to creating good strokes.

Note: Using the appropriate balls and rackets with young kids can make a huge difference in the development of the strokes. Foam balls are the best choice for young players because regular tennis balls bounce higher. The higher bounce causes them to change their grips to accommodate the contact point. Using the appropriate length and weight of the racket can have an impact on the grip. If either the ball or the racket is inappropriate for their age or size, students will often start using an extreme grip or *under grip*. This can limit the strokes production and the development of the player.

There are single-handed grips and double or two-handed grips. There are fewer players that use the single-handed backhand as it takes more power to control and juniors are starting to play tennis at a much younger age. In some rare cases, the player will have two-handed grips on both sides. Using these grips effectively can become complicated when switching hands to hit the ball on either side. It will limit the reach and is not recommended in teaching to beginners.

Different Grips

There are several different grips used in hitting the strokes. Most grips are taught, but some of the grips develop over time due to the height of the player, the surface that is played on, the technique used and the individual style of the player. In explaining the various grips and exact position of the hands on the racket handle, you can use the bevels on the grip and the pressure points on the base of the hand and the trigger finger. The grip of the racket is made up of eight sides, as seen in the picture. They can be numbered from 1 to 8 to properly indicate the sides that make contact with the pressure points of the hands. The pressure points on the hand, points A and B, are indicated in the picture below

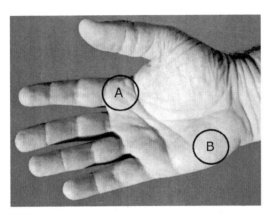 

The Continental Grip

With this grip, you can hit the ball flat, slice, or with slight spin. It can be advantageous with fast returns of the forehand and backhand and with balls played on the rise. As long as the ball stays low, the player can play fairly fast with these grips. In today's game, with the change of equipment and strings, the ball has a lot more spin that makes the ball bounce higher. This grip does not lend itself well to play topspin or play against topspin since the contact points are farther back and there is less power transfer from the body. For juniors, I would not recommend these grips because of the contact point, relative higher bounce of the ball, and the height of the player.

- Continental Forehand

  A is on side 2
  B is on side 1 and 2

- Continental Backhand

  A is on side 2
  B is on side 1

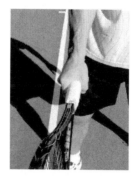

- Continental Backhand
  Double-handed

  R Hand: A on side 2 and 3
               B on side 2

  L Hand: A is on side 3
               B is on side 3

The Eastern Grip

This is one of the most commonly used grips with beginning tennis players. It is easy to use and has little limitations in its use. With the angle of the wrist and the hand on the racket, the weight of the body is behind the ball at impact. This grip lends itself well to drive through the ball or play with some spin for control. There is flexibility to make some adjustments in contact points for low- or high-bouncing balls.

- Eastern Forehand

  A is on side 3
  B is on side 3

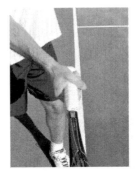

- Eastern Backhand

  A is on side 1 and 2
  B is on side 1

- Easter Backhand
  Double-handed

  R Hand: A on side 1 and 2
             B on side 1

  L Hand: A is on side 3
             B is on side 3

Martin van Daalen

The Semi-western and Western Grip

These grips are most suitable in teaching juniors, especially the semi-western grip. With their smaller height and the bounce of the ball, the kids have an easier time at contacting the ball in front and at shoulder height. Wide shots and low shots in front can be a discomfort due to the restrictions of the wrist turning forward with this grip.

- Semi-western Forehand

    A is on side 3 and 4
    B is on side 3

- Western Forehand

    A is on side 4
    B is on side 4 and 5

As you can see in the pictures, the grips are viewed from both side of the body. The Semi-western forehand and the western forehand are the most used by juniors. For adults, it is advisable to start by using the eastern forehand grip. Observe how the contact point moves forward of the body as the grip changes from continental grip to the western grip. With the under grip, the contact point moves slightly back again with the elbow being bent at contact to accommodate the racket angle at impact with the ball. Note the angle of the arm and the racket and the changes with each grip.

Under Grip

With the hand and trigger finger placed mostly under the grip, the power transfer forward to the ball can be problematic. This grip is common with young juniors when they have not been taught to adjust the feet and hit the ball lower between the hip and the shoulder. The racket head speed has to be much faster to get the same results as the other grips. Making clean contact can be difficult at times, especially on wide shots and low-bouncing (slice) balls.

- Under Grip

  A is on side 5
  B is on side 4 and 5

Backhand Grips

There are many varieties possible with both hands used on the backhand. We need to consider the grips of both hands. A right-handed player's right-hand grip can range from in front of the racket to a western grip. The left hand can vary from a continental grip to an under grip. To teach beginning players, I would start with an eastern backhand grip on the right hand and a semi-western forehand grip on the left hand. These grips are most commonly used and are the most comfortable during play.

Switching Grips

Changing grips from forehand to backhand and vice versa is a confusing process at first. There are ways to teach this and simplify the action. Catching the racket on the follow through from the forehand plays an important role in making the change. Catching the racket with the left hand on the throat of the racket establishes the contact with the supporting hand. In returning to the ready position, the left hand supports the racket. With the backswing from the backhand, the right hand has the opportunity to release the grip and slide over to the backhand grip. With a double-handed backhand, the left hand slides down the throat of the racket until both hands touch. After the follow through, the hands will return in front of the body to the starting position.

Dominant Hand with Backhands

Most players have a dominant hand when playing the backhand. They either favor the right hand or left hand in hitting the backhand. Being right-handed or left-handed does not always determine the dominant hand in double-handed backhands. A more telltale sign is the force they use with either the left or right hand. There are some players who coordinate the force between the two hands and start the stroke with the power from the front arm and drive it through with the power from the back arm. A good example of this method is Andre Agassi. So as a coach, how do you determine this with your player? *An easy detection method is to have your student hit separately with each arm.* If one arm is dominant, they will not be very comfortable with the other arm. If both arms are pretty equal, they use both arms with the backhand. Using this method for training is an excellent way to enhance coordination and control for the double-handed backhand!

Impact of the Grips on the Swing

- **Backswing**
  The different grips of the strokes will affect the shape of the backswing. With kids starting younger and the change of racket construction and strings, the grips have moved more to western or semi-western grips.

  The continental grip has a flat oval shape or even a straight backswing. Normally, the backswing will become more circular in nature as it moves from a continental grip toward a western (see picture below).

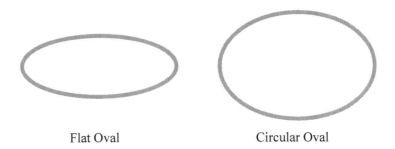

Flat Oval   Circular Oval

- **Racket Trajectory**
  The swing path of the racket changes with different grips. The swing path is the racket trajectory from the backswing to the follow through. This path changes mechanically because of the different angle of the wrist on the racket and how it has to line up to make contact with the ball. The start of the backswing initiates the change in racket trajectory (see picture).

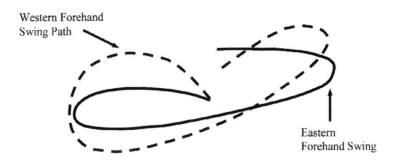

Western Forehand Swing Path

Eastern Forehand Swing

- **Distance to Contact**
  Because of the different grips, the angle of the wrist on the racket will change the contact point with the ball. The continental grip will have a contact point at the side of the body or just in front. The contact point moves away from the body as the ball is hit at a higher contact point. As the grips move from continental to eastern, semi-western, and western grips, the contact point moves more in front of the body. With the under-grip however, the elbow is not fully stretched at contact. This causes the under grip to have a contact point less in front than a western grip (see picture on the right).

Martin van Daalen

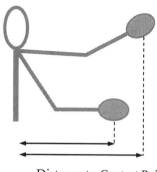

Distance to Contact Point   Contact in Front

- **Follow Through**

    As we stated earlier, racket trajectory changes with different grips. With the follow through being part of this trajectory as well, it changes its path in the height and finish of the follow through. The continental grip has a lower follow through than with a western grip that follows through higher in front of the player. The finish of the western grip, however, might be lower (see picture racket trajectory).

- **Effects of the Grips on the Strokes**

    The execution of the strokes is affected with different grips. All grips have some advantages and disadvantages in their use. The angle of the wrist and the position of the hand on the grip make certain shots either very easy to hit or very difficult to execute. Advanced players will adjust the grip slightly or change it altogether in order to execute the shot to their advantage. A good example is a slice backhand retrieved from a wide-angle shot. The player will slide the grip from a continental grip to an eastern forehand grip in order to open the angle of the racket to slide the strings underneath the ball. Players should adjust grips to their shot choice.

Note: Although you would not teach these advanced techniques to beginning players, as a coach it is useful to observe players to see if they show signs of making these adjustments themselves. Often, when you see players make these adjustments, they show signs of intuitive talent in movement and control of the ball and racket.

Grip Development

As discussed before, the development of proper grips is essential in tennis. The first experience in learning how to grip the racket is usually a lasting experience. But it can change in the initial learning phase and needs to be corrected and observed right from the start. It is very problematic and time-consuming to change grips at a later stage. It often leads to a loss of confidence and causes confusion in how to hit the ball. When analyzing the grips, there are some teaching tips and error detection methods you can use.

- **Forehand Grip:** An easy way to teach students how to grip the racket in a forehand grip is to hold the racket straight in front and shake hands with the grip of the racket. Make sure there is a separation with the index finger, or trigger finger, and the rest of the fingers (the base of the hand and the index finger will be on side 3). Another method is to lay the racket flat on the ground. The student then place their flat hand on the racket and picks it up. The grips are best described by the illustration on the left. The octagon has the same shape as the butt cap of a racket and the sides are numbered to identify them. For example, 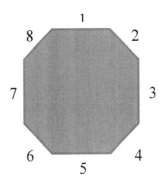 a right-handed eastern forehand grip: the base of the hand and the index finger will both be on side 2.

As you can see in the pictures above, the forehand grip is just like shaking hands with the grip of the racket. The students start with an open hand on the strings of the racket (see picture on the left). Slide the open hand down the racket (see picture on the right) till the base of the hand is on the butt of the racket. Finally shake hands with the grip of the racket and have the trigger finger forward with some space between the trigger finger and the middle finger. The thumb creates a "lock" with the middle finger and wraps around the grip just above the middle finger. Grips should be held firm, but never squeeze too hard. A good way to gauge that is the pressure of the grip from 1 to 10, with 10 being the highest. Grip pressure 5 or 6 is the correct grip pressure.

- **Backhand Grip:** A method to teach the backhand grip is to hold the racket flat and parallel to the ground at shoulder height. A right-handed player will grip the racket handle with the right hand and a straight arm. The base of the hand will be on side 1 and the base of the index finger will be on side 2. If double-handed, the left hand joins the right hand above the right hand with a straight arm. The base of the hand and the index finger will both be on side 7.

As you can see in the pictures above, the backhand grip can be formed by holding the racket at shoulder height and gripping the racket with the base of the hand on the butt cap. The racket should be held square to the ground to ensure the proper grip. The trigger finger wraps around the grip with a space between the trigger finger and the middle finger. The thumb creates a lock with the middle finger and is positioned just above the middle finger. Grip pressure should be firm without squeezing too hard. You can check if players are comfortable with the backhand grip by having them bounce a ball upward at shoulder height.

- **The Service Grip:** A method in teaching the service grip is to hold the racket straight in front of the player, on top of the racket handle, just like holding a hammer (continental forehand grip). The base of the hand should be on the sides of racket between the top and slanted sides of the racket handle, sides 1 and 2. This is the most comfortable service grip for beginning players to make contact with the ball. The base of the index finger will be on side 2.

- Service Grip

  A is on side 2
  B is on side 1 and 2

- **The Volley Grip:** The method is the same as the service grip. The differences in the forehand and backhand volley are the continental forehand grip for the forehand volley and the continental backhand grip for the backhand volley. This to accommodate the comfort and power transfer for the player. With the forehand volley, the base of the hand will be between side 1 and 2, and the base of the index finger will be on side 2. With the backhand volley, the base of the hand will be on side 1 and the base of the index finger will be on side 2.

Error detection of grips during baseline play is possible by paying attention to the contact points of the strokes. When stepping forward to make contact with forehand or backhand, the contact points should be at the front foot or preferably just in front of the front foot. The shoulders have to rotate and the arms have to stretch to accommodate this position of contact. The wrist angle (preferably around a forty-five-degree angle with the racket) and hand position will support an efficient power transfer from the body to the ball. Look for a smooth follow through and wrist stability through contact to maintain good grips over time. A bent elbow at contact with the ball is a possible indication of an improper grip and/or contact point.

- **Error detection of grips with the service action** starts with observing the contact point, wrist position at impact with the ball, and the follow through. Most beginning players have trouble with the service grip and ball toss when starting to learn the motion. The ball toss might be off-line and need some practice first. When tossing the ball too far in front the grip will tend to slide to a western grip. Sometimes, you will even see the thumb disconnect from the ring finger and slide on top of the grip, as if holding a frying pan. If the toss of the ball is straight in front of the body, the shoulders cannot swing around to comfortably make contact with the ball. The player will change the grip in order to position the shoulder and the racket with the contact point of the ball.

- **Error detection of grips with the volley action** is a combination of factors. Look at the contact points, the racket trajectory and the wrist action. If you see the arm and the racket at the side of the body during contact point and the racket head dipping downward right after contact, there is usually a cause to check the grip.

- **Avoiding bad grips** is possible by paying special attention to the fundamentals and habits of your students during play. It is especially important to watch for the contact points of the strokes when working with beginning players. Carefully look at the contact points in front of the body as well as the distance and height of the contact point. Consistency with the contact points in all three dimensions is the key to proper grip development.

Prevent students from hitting high balls above their shoulders on forehand and backhand. Make a correction by having the players back up and hit the ball at a lower contact point. Proper contact points are between hip and shoulder. To play the balls above their shoulders will eventually change their grips (see under grip).

Avoid running less experienced players over the court too much. Players will hit the balls at the side of the body (late hits), flip their wrist, and change their grips. Players need to make all movements to the ball in a controlled fashion to maintain proper contact points. It will save you invaluable time later.

Avoid players (or coaches) trying to hit too hard. It will be the cause of bad grip development by hitting the ball late or at the side of the body. The players will try to make adjustments and make grip changes or wrist adjustments that lead to bad stroke development.

Good grips are the foundation of any good stroke production.

Serena and Venus Williams

Martin van Daalen

STROKE PRODUCTION

When teaching strokes, a coach should know the difference between the fundamentals and the style of a player in order to give the proper instruction.

Fundamentals

These are the basic technical principles to hit the stroke (see key positions below). All players have fundamentals although not exactly the same ones. Example: Not every player has the same contact point for a particular stroke. However, they do have to hit it at a consistent point in relation to the body that fits with the other fundamentals of the stroke for it to be effective and reliable. The contact point is one of the fundamentals, but the way it is executed within the stroke is the style of the player.

Style

This is a personal expression of the stroke. Many players have different styles in hitting the ball, even as a junior. Example: Roger Federer has similar fundamentals to Pete Sampras, as he modeled his game after Pete's, as a junior. They each have a very distinctive style with differences in how they strike the ball. The fundamentals and individual style has developed them both to be very effective players.

Key Positions

The key positions are like a "freeze-frame point" during a stroke that indicates a certain part of the stroke. They all have an important impact on how the stroke is performed. Grips have a very high impact on the execution and swing path of the stroke. The key positions, together with grips, make up the fundamentals of the stroke. The key positions are made up of seven different positions within the stroke. These seven positions are:

1. Ready position
2. Backswing
3. Loading
4. Forward swing
5. Contact point
6. Follow through
7. Recovery

The key positions are not exactly the same for every player. The variations of one key position will lead to differences in other positions of the stroke. The grips and shot choice of the player will lead to changes in the backswing, contact points, and follow through. They all work together within the mechanics and the style of the player to be consistent and reliable. Key positions are elemental in looking for errors in the stroke production! Make sure you are aware of the particular shot choice and grips before making judgment on a correction or instruction. To study the key positions properly, you need to videotape the stroke production. Make sure to take several shots from the same stroke to see if they vary. Also take the shots from different angles (side, back, and front) to make sure the player's body does not block your view of the stroke.

KEY POSITIONS OF THE FOREHAND

Ready Position

- Athletic posture
- Hands relaxed
- Knees slightly bent
- Split step
- Alert disposition

Backswing

- Shoulder rotate with racket
- Hips rotate outside
- Toe turns outside
- Racket swing back

Loading

- Placing outer foot
- Turning hips
- Turning shoulders
- Extending both arm
- Balance arm to side

Martin van Daalen

Forward Swing

- Unloading legs
- Unloading hips
- Unloading shoulders
- Tracking oncoming ball
- Lining up racket path

Contact Point

- Squaring the shoulders
- Stability in wrist
- Weight transfer
- Accelerate through contact

Follow Through

- Arm forward and around
- Foot skips around
- Full turn of the hips
- Full turn of the shoulders
- Accelerate follow through

Recovery

- Recovery footwork
- Overstep outside foot
- Racket back in front
- Positioning body to cover the court

Teaching the Forehand with Key Positions

In teaching beginning players, you can use the key positions as a guideline in building the forehand. The progression from ready position to recovery makes you go from start to finish of the stroke without skipping any steps. Introduce the whole stroke first and show what it is supposed to look like before getting into specifics.

Note: Always use a progression in teaching any topic—consistency first, then depth, followed by direction or change of direction. Don't move on to the next progression before it is improved sufficiently with control.

1. *Start with the "whole method" first before breaking it down in parts.* The students can start with mini tennis and work their way back to the baseline as long as they show control with the ball. Find exercises in consistency, depth, and direction. Using the semi-western grip gives the most flexibility in developing the strokes.

2. *Stabilize the contact points next.* This stabilizes the stroke before you start working on specifics. It also prevents the stroke from breaking down or having to correct too many things at the same time. Points to look for as a coach: The squaring off of the hips and shoulders at point of contact. Remember that different grips result in different contact points and shoulder positions.

3. *The ready position is the position of the body before any rally is started.* It needs to be consistent in execution and flow into the split step. The ready position should be an athletic position, relaxed but alert in anticipation of the action to follow. Proper tension of the muscles (relaxed) assists the speed of the split step before the action. Let your students feel the difference of how much faster they can move when they are in a relaxed, athletic position. The balance hand supports the racket.

4. *The backswing is performed as a unit-turn to the side where the ball will be struck.* The placement of the outside foot initiates the movement. The hips, shoulders, arms, and racket all turn in coordination with the swing. The arms and racket together make a flat oval-shaped backswing

Martin van Daalen

that slows down at the side of the body in order to load the stroke. The supporting hand lets go of the throat of the racket and stretches out to the side of the body. The hitting arm is slightly bent at the elbow as it separates farther from the balance arm. You can practice this motion with your students after showing them the example. (You can create the flat oval shape by holding your racket horizontally next to their body and have them swing around it.)

5. *Loading the body in preparation for the stroke is a difficult concept for beginning and intermediate tennis players.* They don't yet feel how the larger muscle groups of the legs and trunk allow the shoulders and arms to relax. The legs, trunk, shoulders, and arm muscles get stretched (loading). This stretching of the muscles creates a tension in the muscles, which is released (unloading) at the time of the forward swing. In teaching this concept, show what the load looks like and feels like. You can use foam balls to illustrate the feeling of the swing becoming faster with the proper loading of the muscles. Foam balls are ideal for this purpose and are really light and soft.

Note: The load is also created by the stored kinetic energy (gravity) by raising the arms and racket up in the backswing. The weight of the arm and racket will accelerate the motion forward. The flat oval shape of the backswing is an important factor in the loading, unloading, and acceleration of the swing. This, in contrast with a straight backswing, where the motion stops at the end of the backswing and has to be restarted in the forward swing (loss of energy, loading, and acceleration).

6. *The forward swing is the initiating part of the swing.* Even though it is called the forward swing, the actual swing starts with a farther-backward stretch of the hitting arm and racket and a dropping motion as it follows the oval shape of the swing. The player uses the gravity on the arm and racket to accelerate the swing. The unloading of the forward swing starts with the step forward toward the ball and the balance arm swinging forward. The hips and shoulders unload and turn forward in the hitting direction. This part of the swing is also responsible for the timing of the swing. The timing of the forward swing comes with experience. Practice this timing with your students by counting and saying 1 at the bounce of the ball and 2 at the moment of impact

with the ball. This method will assist in the timing and rhythm of the swing.

7. *The contact point is the point of impact from the racket with the ball in relation to the body.* The ideal contact point for the forehand should be between hip and shoulder and in front of the body, leveled with the front foot. The shoulder position should be square at impact with the racket (see picture). Coordinating both feet to the proper distance and height of the contact points is crucial to the development of the strokes.

8. *The follow through is the finish of the stroke after contact with the ball.* It can assist in controlling the flight path. This part of the swing needs to be extended forward, around the body, and slightly upward. Teaching the follow through can be simplified by catching the racket with the balance arm, just under the racket head, above the other shoulder. This motion solves a lot of mechanical errors without having to teach them separately. Students can pose at the end of the stroke to check the follow through.

9. *The recovery is the movement back to the ready position to cover the court in preparation for the next shot.* With the step forward into the ball, players recover by bringing the back foot forward next to the other foot and squaring off the feet in the hitting direction. This recovery creates the ready position for the next stroke. With the open-stance positions, the recovery is much more complicated and needs to be taught when the players are more advanced. Teaching open-stance positions too early in the development makes the footwork lazy and sloppy. The students will have difficulty learning the weight transfer and can develop technical errors that take a long time to correct.

Martin van Daalen

KEY POSITIONS OF THE BACKHAND

Ready Position

- Athletic posture
- Hands relaxed
- Knees slightly bent
- Split step
- Alert disposition

Backswing

- Shoulder rotate with racket
- Hips rotate outside
- Toe turns outside
- Racket swing back

Loading

- Placing front foot
- Turning hips
- Turning shoulders
- Raising both arms

Martin van Daalen

Forward Swing

- Unloading legs
- Unloading hips
- Unloading shoulders
- Tracking oncoming ball
- Lining up racket path

Contact Point

- Before front foot
- Stability in wrist
- Weight transfer
- Accelerate through contact

Follow Through

- Arm forward and around
- Foot skips around
- Full turn of the hips
- Full turn of the shoulders
- Finish over the other shoulder

Recovery

- Recovery footwork
- Overstep outside foot
- Positioning body to cover the court

KEY POSITIONS OF THE DOUBLE-HANDED BACKHAND

Ready Position

- Athletic posture
- Hands relaxed
- Knees slightly bent
- Split step
- Alert disposition

Backswing

- Shoulder rotate with racket
- Hips rotate outside
- Toe turns outside
- Racket swing back

Loading

- Placing front foot
- Turning hips
- Turning shoulders
- Raising both arms

Martin van Daalen

Forward Swing

- Unloading legs
- Unloading hips
- Unloading shoulders
- Tracking oncoming ball
- Lining up racket path

Contact Point

- Before front foot
- Stability in wrist
- Weight transfer
- Accelerate through contact

Follow Through

- Arm forward and around
- Foot skips around
- Full turn of the hips
- Full turn of the shoulders

Recovery

- Recovery footwork
- Overstep outside foot
- Positioning body to cover the court

Teaching the Backhand with Key Positions

Using the key positions to teach the double-handed backhand is an essential tool for coaches, players, and parents. Beginning players need to be instructed by using a progression of teaching. The key positions are an excellent way to introduce all the details of the stroke. They become important to the player as they improve and want to excel. The double-handed backhand has very simple mechanics in comparison to other strokes and is relatively easy to learn and teach.

Note: Follow the progression of consistency first, then depth, followed by direction or change of direction. Don't move on to the next progression before it is improved significantly with control and consistency.

1. *Start with the "whole method" before breaking it down in details.* Begin with mini tennis and work your way back to the baseline. Continue to move back to the baseline, as long as the players show they have control over the ball. Find exercises in consistency, depth and direction. Using the eastern backhand grip provides the most stability to the wrist. For double-handed backhands add the semi-western grip of the supporting hand and bring both hands close together at the bottom of the grip.

2. *Stabilize the contact points next.* This stabilizes the stroke before you start working on specifics. The hips and shoulders are slightly open at contact. The shoulders do not square off as much as the forehand at contact point, but do square off with the follow through. The contact point of the one-handed backhand will be more in front of the body than the double-handed backhand. The hips need to rotate through contact to obtain more power, consistency, and stability in making contact with the ball. This is accomplished with timely preparation, good footwork, and hitting the ball out in front of the body.

3. *The ready position is the stance of the body in preparation for action.* It should be an athletic position—relaxed but alert in anticipation of the action to follow. Proper tension of the muscles (relaxed) assists the speed of the split step before the action. Both arms are in a relaxed position with the elbows loose in front of the body. The balance hand supports the racket just under the racket head.

4. *The backswing is performed as a unit-turn to the side where the ball will be struck.* The placement of the outside foot initiates the movement. The hips, shoulders, and the arms and racket all turn in coordination of the swing. The arms and racket together make a flat oval-shaped backswing and slow down at the side of the body in order to load the body. In the backswing, the grip change takes place with the bottom hand. With the double-handed backhand, the supporting hand lets go of the throat of the racket and slides down to join the other hand on the grip. Both arms are slightly bent at the elbow. The racket is tilted upward in a forty-five-degree angle. You can practice this motion with your students after showing them the example. Create the flat oval shape by holding a racket horizontally next to their body and have them swing around it.

5. *Loading the body begins with turning the shoulders backward and placing the front foot toward the ball.* The muscles and ligaments from the legs, trunk, shoulders, and arms get stretched. The elasticity creates the stored energy we call loading. This tension can be released (unloading) with the forward swing. Players can feel this concept by using foam balls and swinging faster without squeezing the racket too hard. The shoulders will turn farther back with a single-handed backhand than with a double-handed backhand with less restriction from the other hand on the grip. The loading is generated just before the forward swing to store the kinetic energy from the gravity of the arms and racket.

Note: The load is created by the stored kinetic energy (gravity) by raising the arms and racket up in the backswing. The weight of the arm and racket will accelerate the motion forward. The flat oval shape of the backswing is an important factor in the loading, unloading, and acceleration of the swing. This is in contrast with the straight backswing. The motion stops at the end of the backswing and has to be initiated in the forward swing (loss of loading and acceleration).

6. *The forward swing is the initiating part of the swing.* Even though it is called the forward swing, the actual swing starts with the backward stretch of both arms and a downward motion of the racket as it follows the oval shape of the swing. The player uses the stored energy from the loading and gravity of the arms and racket to accelerate the swing.

The unloading of the forward swing begins with the step forward toward the ball. The shoulders partially unload and turn forward in the hitting direction. With the double-handed backhand the arms coordinate together in producing the forward swing. The front arm uses the pulling/rotating action to get the motion started while the back arm and hand take over just before contact with the ball in providing the forward-pushing action. With a single-handed backhand, the supporting hand lets go of the racket and the forward swing is initially generated with the unloading of the front shoulder turn.

7. *The contact point is the point of impact from the racket with the ball in relation to the body.* The ideal contact point for the backhand should be between hip and shoulder and in front of the body, leveled with the front foot. The shoulder position is slightly open at impact with the ball. With the double-handed backhand, the shoulders will be slightly more open (see picture). Coordinating the movement of the feet for proper distance and height to the contact point is crucial to the development of the strokes.

8. *The follow through is the finish of the stroke after making contact with the ball.* It can assist in controlling the flight path. This part of the swing needs to be extended forward, around the body, and slightly upward. Teaching the follow through can be simplified by finishing the hand(s) above the other shoulder. By using this method there will be an automated bend of the arm(s) in the follow through. The hips and shoulders will rotate farther to finally square off to the hitting direction. Even as a one-handed player, it can be beneficial to practice the follow through with two hands to feel the finish of the stroke above the other shoulder. Have the students pose at the end of the stroke to check the follow through.

9. *The recovery is the movement back to the ready position to cover the court in preparation of the next shot.* With the step toward the ball, players recover by bringing the back foot forward next to the other foot. With the open-stance positions, the recovery is much more complicated and needs to be taught when the players are more advanced. Teaching open-stance positions too early in the development makes the stroke very mechanical and forced. The students do not learn to use their weight transfer and can develop some technical errors that take a long time to correct.

KEY POSITIONS OF THE SERVE

Ready Position

- Bouncing of the ball (rhythm)
- Arms relaxed
- Weight transfer to back foot
- Back knee bend
- Arms swing up slightly

Backswing

- Separation of both arms
- Weight transfer forward
- Shoulder turn
- Hip turn
- Hips forward for balance

Loading

- Bending knees farther
- Turning hips
- Turning shoulders
- Hips out in front for power
  And balance

Forward Swing

- Straightening (unloading) legs
- Racket drops between shoulders
- Turning of hips and shoulders
- Extending arm up and forward
- Balance arm drops to stomach

Contact Point

- Hand in front
- Swing upward
- Tossing arm in stomach
- Extension of the wrist

Follow Through

- Outward turn of the wrist
- Extending arm
- Upward kick back foot
- Landing on left foot
- Posture upper body

Recovery

- Back foot recovery in front
- Recovery footwork backward
- Positioning body for next shot

Teaching the Service Action with Key Positions

The serve is a complicated and coordinated motion to execute. Both arms move separately in opposite directions with a different purpose. When teaching beginning tennis players, keep in mind that they are not able to perform the same actions that advanced players can perform. The knee, hip, and shoulder actions will also not be as prominent as it would be with more experienced players. Therefore it is advisable to take it slow when teaching the service action. Most often, the students themselves will show when they are ready to take the next step. The fluidity in the stroke improves together with more consistency and direction. That will be the time to further develop the specifics of the service action. Until that time, stabilizing the service action with the key positions will be very helpful to their development.

Note: Follow the progression of consistency first, followed in this case by direction. The depth of the serve is not an issue yet with beginning and intermediate players. Don't move on to the next progression before it is improved sufficiently.

1. *Start with the "whole method" before breaking it down to details.* The students can start at the service line (especially with really young players) and work their way back to the baseline. Don't move back to the next spot until they show the control over the ball. At this level, try to find exercises in consistency and direction for improvement. The continental grip is recommended because it provides the wrist with the most stability in the service action.

2. *Stabilize the toss of the ball and the contact point next.* The toss determines the contact point of the serve. Stabilize the toss of the ball before you start working on specifics. The balance of the body, in this phase, plays a crucial part in the execution of the motion. As a coach, you need to observe if the hips are out in front to maintain the balance during the loading phase. The hips and shoulders rotate forward to make contact just in front of the body.

3. *The ready position of the serve is a point of relaxation before the action.* The player may bounce the ball a few times to focus and find a rhythm. The ball is in the top of the thumb, index finger, and middle finger. The other two fingers support the racket so that both arms are in a relaxed stretched position. The bodyweight is mostly on the front foot before the loading of the swing. The feet are in a closed stance with the line through the top of the toes pointing toward the hitting direction. As the players become more advanced, the position of the feet is turned more sideways from the net.

4. *The backswing is a combination of the toss of the ball and the backswing with the upward motion of the hitting arm and racket.* Both arms swing to a Y-position (see picture). The toss needs to be straight up, out of the top of the fingers, and slightly to the side. You can teach the accuracy of the toss by having the students toss the ball in the air and let it land on the ground. The ball should land in line with the front foot. The back arm swings above the shoulder and bends at the elbow. In the backswing, the hand opens up as it passes by the hips before the racket drops down between the shoulder blades. The bodyweight shifts from the front foot to the back foot. The shoulders turn sideways and slightly farther than parallel with the sidelines (this to accommodate the outward shoulder turn on the forward swing). As the players advance, the hand will not open in the backswing and will aid in keeping the elbow up (see *Teaching Advanced Tennis Volume 2*).

5. *Loading of the service motion is different with beginning and intermediate players and even more so with experienced players.* Beginning tennis players will use less loading of the shoulders and hips, and the knee bend is minimal. The loading of the serve is accomplished by the backswing, the weight shift, the turn of the shoulders, and the knee action. The loading of the backswing occurs by bringing the racket above the hand at the end of the swing and then dropping the racket in between the shoulder blades. This dropping of the arm, just before power is applied, accelerates the forward swing. The forward weight shift helps the turn of the knees and shoulders. The shoulder turn in the backswing loads the shoulder just before power is applied to the forward swing. Intermediate players will start using more hip and knee action. The knee bend loads the knees to start the motion

from the ground up. The knee bend is at its deepest point at the end of the backswing. This loading of the three components needs to be coordinated with each other in order to keep the balance.

6. *The forward swing starts as the knees extend upward.* The rotation follows from the hips up to the shoulders in opening forward to the direction of the ball. The unloading of the knees to the hips and shoulders, the hitting arm, the elbow, and at last, the wrist is the kinetic chain that transfers the power from the ground up. The upward motion of the knees activates the racket to drop even lower between the shoulder blades. The weight or mass of the racket and the acceleration of the upward and forward motion of the arm and shoulders creates the lag of the racket head. The lag in the arm, elbow, and the wrist as it follows the hips and shoulders, supplies the acceleration to the racket head. The balance arm drops from the toss position down to the waist to later catch the racket in the follow through.

7. *The contact point of the serve is in front of the body.* The point of impact needs to be where the arm can be stretched so the racket can hit the ball in a relaxed fashion. If the toss is too low, the arm will not reach a stretched position and the wrist and racket head will become unstable. If the toss is too high, the timing of the ball becomes a problem. The ball will hang in the air too long, and the motion has to stop or slow down too much to create a fluid motion. The hips and shoulders turn forward to meet the ball and are almost square with the hitting direction at the moment of impact. The eyes should be focused on the ball, during contact, to swing up and ensure a clean hit service action.

8. *The follow through of the serve is the motion with the racket swinging through the ball to the other side of the body.* The balance arm goes from the toss position to a bent position in front of the stomach to clear the path for the racket on the follow through. This motion of the balance arm assists the rotation of the body in hitting the ball and maintaining the balance during the stroke. At the end of the follow through, the balance arm will catch the racket as it passes the other side of the body, near the hip. The shoulders continue the rotation and bring the hips along. The back leg will finish with the rotating of the leg and the foot on the top of the toe. As the service motion becomes faster, the finish of the service action will change.

Martin van Daalen

9. *The recovery of the service action restores the balance after the swing and makes it possible to get ready for the next stroke.* The faster the service action, the more the momentum will carry the bodyweight beyond the front foot. After the jump and skip of the front foot, the back foot will step through to stabilize the body and step back after the follow through. This stabilizing motion needs to be practiced in order to maintain your balance. The arms swing back in front of the body in order to restore the ready position. The player moves back behind the baseline and can prepare for the next stroke.

KEY POSITIONS OF THE FOREHAND VOLLEY

Ready Position

- Athletic posture
- Hands relaxed
- Knees slightly bent
- Split step forward
- Alert disposition

Backswing

- Wrist flex backward
- Hips rotate outside
- Toe turns outside
- Short backswing

Loading

- Bending knees farther
- Weight on back foot
- Turning hips
- Turning shoulders
- Balance arm to side

Martin van Daalen

Forward Swing

- Unloading legs (step)
- Unloading hips
- Unloading shoulders
- Tracking oncoming ball
- Lining up racket path

Contact Point

- Hand in front
- Stability in wrist
- Weight transfer
- Hitting zone

Follow Through

- Arm extended
- Weight transfer
- Wrist position
- Balance

Recovery

- Skip of the back foot
- Split step
- Positioning to cover the court

Teaching the Forehand Volley with Key Positions

The forehand volley is generally a simple action but is often made more complicated than needed. Teaching the volley can be simplified by catching the ball with your hand instead of using the racket. Players will lose some of the fear of being closer to the net. It teaches them to make automated movements in adjusting to the ball by bending the knees and catching the ball out in front of the body (players will automatically try to catch the ball at eye level). The coach can throw or feed the balls left and right from them, or even straight at them, to make them aware how to move out of the way. Creating the same position when catching the ball is the key to solid and consistent volleys.

Note: Follow the progression of consistency first, then depth, followed by direction or change of direction. Don't move on to the next progression before it is improved sufficiently.

1. *Catching the ball first before trying the volley action with the racket is the preferred method in the progression.* Try to make it as easy as possible at first and then venture out to more movement and speed in catching the ball. Moving a little farther back can make it even more difficult. Teach the continental grip for the forehand volley.

2. *Stabilize the contact points by blocking the ball at impact point with the ball.* This stabilizes the stroke as a whole before you start working on specifics. It trains the arm and the wrist to strengthen and to hold that position of the racket head for control. It also instills in the students to hit the volley with their legs, by stepping forward, instead of swinging the racket.

3. *The ready position for the volley is the preparation to move in either direction to the ball.* The elbows are loose and in front of the body. The balance arm holds the racket lightly with the fingers just under the racket head. The balance of the body is slightly forward on the balls of the feet to step in toward the ball. The ready position flows into the split step when the opponent strikes the ball.

Martin van Daalen

4. *The backswing of the volley is short and simple.* After the split step, the wrist turns sideways and backward so the racket is in position to "punch" the ball. The supporting hand lets go of the racket and stays in front of the body for balance during the stroke. The back foot moves first behind the oncoming ball to create the proper distance. The knees are bent to accommodate the height of the ball. The hitting arm is slightly bent at the elbow, as the shoulders turn slightly sideways. The racket is held at a forty-five-degree angle with the ground at the end of the backswing.

5. *Loading the body in preparation for the volley is the turn of the shoulders and the bending of the legs.* In teaching this concept, show the players what the load looks like and let them feel the action first. The turn of the shoulders creates the stored energy for the punch with the racket. The knees bend in preparation for the volley to step forward and push the body against the ball. The bending of the knees provides the loading of the legs for the power behind the volley (weight transfer).

6. *The forward swing is initiated with the legs.* The unloading of the forward swing starts with the step forward, toward the ball. The back shoulder turns forward in the hitting direction. The nails of the hand and the racket head keep facing the target as long as possible to enhance the direction of the ball. The balance arm turns with the motion of the shoulders but stays in front of the body for balance during the stroke. Maintaining the angle of the wrist keeps the volley crisp at contact. Allow players to feel this weight transfer and unloading of the legs by standing in front of them and applying pressure against the hand. They will be able to feel the difference in power when standing straight up or using the knees. The same goes with the racket in front or at the side. The speed of the forward step will influence the speed of the ball.

7. *The contact point is the point of impact from the racket with the ball in relation to the body.* The ideal contact point for the forehand volley should be level with the front foot but does vary some with the height of the ball. The shoulder position should be almost square with the racket head at impact. Beginning players can learn how to find this contact point by blocking the ball at impact and keeping the racket in the same angle. Moving the body in the proper position behind the ball takes practice and experience. The knees play a crucial part in lining

up the eyes as much as possible with the ball. Keeping the angle of the racket with the wrist stable improves the consistency and direction.

8. *The follow through is the finish of the stroke after contact with the ball.* It can help in controlling the depth and direction of the ball. The elbow is extended forward with the racket head facing the target. The follow through is short and direct. The players pose at the end of the stroke to check the follow through.

9. *The recovery of the stroke is to recover the balance after the swing and to prepare for the next shot.* With the step forward into the ball, you want to recover by bringing the back foot forward next to the other foot and squaring off the feet. This recovery creates the ready position to move for the next stroke. The body repositions and the players react to the next volley or overhead.

Martin van Daalen

Ready Position

- Athletic posture
- Hands relaxed
- Knees slightly bent
- Split step
- Alert disposition

Backswing

- Shoulder rotate with racket
- Hips rotate outside
- Back foot steps behind
- Toe turns outside
- Racket swing back

Loading

- Bending knees
- Turning hips
- Turning shoulders
- Extending both arm
- Balance arm to side

Forward Swing

- Unloading legs
- Step forward
- Tracking oncoming ball
- Lining up racket path

Contact Point

- Hand in front
- Stability in wrist
- Weight transfer
- Hitting zone

Follow Through

- Arm extended
- Weight transfer
- Arms separate
- Balance

Recovery

- Recovery footwork
- Back-foot skip
- Repositioning body

Teaching the Backhand Volley with Key Positions

The backhand volley is usually a tougher stroke to master for beginning tennis players because of the lack of wrist strength. With very young players, you could start off using lighter balls or feeding from less distance in practice. The progression of this stroke should still be by catching the ball first and then trying to use the racket by blocking the ball from less distance to control the wrist and the racket. By moving both arms in opposite directions during the stroke, the balance arm will create a counterforce for the hitting arm. The faster the balance arm moves backward, the faster the hitting arm will move in the opposite direction. This concept of action and reaction takes a while to develop and requires strength of the arms to execute. As a coach, you need to know the strength of your students and adjust the intensity of the execution.

Note: Follow the progression of consistency first, then depth, followed by direction or change of direction. Don't move on to the next progression before it is improved sufficiently.

1. *Start to catch the ball before trying the volley action with the racket.* Make it as easy as possible and then venture out to more movement and speed. Moving a little farther back can make it even more difficult. Teach the continental backhand grip for the backhand volley (see chapter on grips).

2. *Stabilize the contact points by stepping in and blocking the ball at impact point with the ball.* This stabilizes the stroke before you start working on specifics. With very young players, use lighter balls or try feeding the ball from less distance. If this is still difficult for them, try letting them use two hands. The contact point should be in front of the body with the arm almost extended at impact. The stability of the wrist controls the direction and depth of the ball.

3. *The ready position for the backhand volley is the preparation to move to either side to the ball.* The elbows are loose and in front of the body. The balance arm holds the racket lightly with the fingers just under the racket head. The balance of the body is slightly forward on the balls

Martin van Daalen

of the feet to step in toward the ball. The ready position flows into the split step when the opponent strikes the ball.

4. *The backswing is short and simple for stability.* The wrist turns sideways and backward so the racket is in position to punch the ball. The supporting hand holds the throat of the racket. With a single-handed volley, the hand lets go of the racket with the forward swing. The back foot moves behind the oncoming ball. The knees are bent to accommodate the height of the ball. The hitting arm is slightly bent at the elbow as the shoulders turn sideways. The racket is held at a forty-five-degree angle with the ground at the end of the backswing.

5. *Loading the body is performed with the turn of the shoulders and the bending of the legs.* In teaching this concept, show students what the load looks like and let them try the action. The turn of the shoulders creates the stored energy for the forward punch. The knees bend in preparation to step forward, against the ball, with the front foot. The bending of the knees provides the power behind the volley (loading).

6. *The forward swing is initiated with the legs.* The unloading of the forward swing starts with the step forward toward the ball. The faster the step forward, the more the ball will speed up. The knuckles of the hand and the racket head keep facing the target as long as possible to enhance the direction of the ball. With the single-handed volley, the balance arm swings backward as a counteraction to provide balance and added power during the stroke. The faster counteraction provides more speed to the racket head. Maintaining the angle of the wrist keeps the volley crisp at contact. The two-handed backhand volley can be used for beginners with less power but is not advised for the development of advanced players with the loss of the reach, power, and balance.

7. *The contact point is the point of impact from the racket with the ball in relation to the body.* The ideal contact point for the backhand volley should be level with the front foot. The shoulders stay sideways, as long as possible, to maintain direction of the ball. Beginning players can learn how to find this contact point by blocking the ball at impact and keeping the racket in the same angle. Moving the body in the proper position behind the ball takes practice and experience. The knees play

a crucial part in maintaining the eyes at level with the ball. Keeping the wrist angle of the racket stable improves consistency and direction.

8. *The follow through is the finish of the stroke after contact with the ball and can assist in controlling the depth and direction of the ball.* The elbow needs to be extended forward with the strings of the racket facing the target. The follow through is short and direct. Hold the pose at the end of the stroke to check the follow through.

9. *The recovery of the volley is to recover the balance after the swing and to prepare for the next shot.* With the step forward into the ball, you want to recover by bringing the back foot forward next to the other foot and squaring off the feet. This recovery creates the ready position to move for the next stroke.

Martin van Daalen

Kim Clijsters

FOOTWORK

With the advancements in equipment and strings, players are hitting the ball harder and earlier after the bounce. Even in junior events, they are striking the ball with more force and are moving faster. This development of the game requires more speed, balance, and recovery in order to cover the whole court. The technique of the footwork needs to be precise and efficient to play faster and to last in long matches.

Some of the advantages of good footwork:

- Better balance before, during, and after the shot.
- Improves control of the ball during the rallies.
- Faster recovery after the shot.
- Better court coverage allows the player to reach more balls.
- More aggressive strokes are possible with better preparation.
- Efficiency of movement helps the preservation of energy.

Stance

There are four different stances to use when positioning your body behind the ball. They all have an impact on the execution and the shot choices of the stroke. The stances are as follows:

1. Closed stance
2. Square stance
3. Semi-open stance
4. Open stance

It bodes well to start novice and less experienced players with the square stance before introducing the semi-open and open stance. When using a square stance, players will feel the improvement of weight transfer and ball control much better. As players improve, weight transfer becomes an important factor for balance and power transfer to the strokes and to apply pressure on the opponent.

Martin van Daalen

Closed Stance

With the feet in this position, it is difficult to turn the shoulders and hips to square the racket at impact with the ball. On the double-handed backhand, it can provide some stability, but on the forehand, it blocks the stroke production of the swing and is not recommended on that side. Set up with the back foot first.

Square Stance

This stance will provide the best weight transfer and rotation of the body while maintaining the balance. The hips and shoulders are able to open up toward the target to square the racket head at impact with the ball. This is the best way to start in teaching beginning tennis players.

Semi-open Stance

This stance can be introduced to intermediate players to enhance the forward rotation of the hips and shoulders. It should also be used to move out of the way to make room for the stroke when the ball is too close to the body.

Open Stance

This stance is not suitable for beginning players and should be reserved for advanced players. Students need to learn the basic footwork and the proper weight transfer first to produce balance and consistency with the ground strokes.

Good strokes are useless without good footwork to get you there.

Movement

On a tennis court, movement needs to be coordinated between the trajectory of the ball and the position of the player. With the different angles, speeds, trajectories, and bounces from the ball, this can prove to be a difficult task.

Martin van Daalen

Direction

You need to be able to move in all directions to place your body in the right position behind the ball. The sideways movement is most common to use, whether it be to the forehand or to the backhand. For balls that fall short in front, use the forward movement. Use the backward movement to retrieve balls that fall deep and/or with a high trajectory.

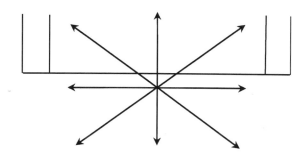

Type of Movement

There are many forms of movement used in tennis for players to be feel balanced and coordinated while playing a rally.

The most common forms of movement:

- Running   - fastest form of movement
- Stepping in or forward   - most used for weight transfer
- Side steps   - with open stance
- Side shuffle   - recovering
- Over step   - to turn in next direction
- Back shuffle   - when positioning behind the ball
- Recover step   - squaring off body for balance
- Skip   - for recovery of balance
- Split step   - starting action before movement

All these types of movement have the sole purpose of maintaining the balance before, during, and after the stroke. The different types of movement are necesarry in order for the player to adjust to the speed, spin, trajectory, and shot choice of the player. It is important to teach these at the appropriate time in sequence with the strokes, the pattern development, and the tactical situations. Try to incorporate this in games and in a competitive setting whenever possible.

Footwork Training

Footwork and stroke production need to be a coordinated effort. Footwork alone will not develop a player. Good strokes require good footwork. There are all sorts of specific drills possible in training each and every one of these movements. Before you start doing any of these, make sure to analyze the movement first. Here are a few tips in starting the footwork and movement for beginning tennis players:

1. Young Juniors (age five to eight)
   At this age, kids move more naturally without conciously thinking about the movement itself. Because of this, the best way to teach footwork is by playing all types of games that promote footwork.

2. Juniors (age eight to twelve)
   This is an ideal age to work on coordinative or rhythm drills and stamina. The technique of the footwork can be introduced in basic forms. Avoid using too many exercises where strength and/or speed are involved because young players may not have sufficient strength. The length of the drills should be kept short. After a short break, you can repeat the drill since their energy returns quickly.

3. Juniors (age twelve to fifteen)
   At this age, the development of footwork becomes more urgent. The kids are becoming stronger, and faster movement is required to keep up with the increasing speeds of the ball. As their legs increase in strength, the recovery footwork becomes important to maintain balance. This age is ideal to enhance the footwork technique, endurance, and consistency in movement.

4. Juniors (age fifteen to eighteen)
   Competition drives the development of all the physical aspects. With their bodies maturing, speed and strength training can be

Martin van Daalen

introduced. Specific footwork and movement training need to be implemented.

Examples of Movement Training for Beginning Players
(In order of progression and difficulty)

- Play up the middle of the court and alternate forehand and backhand strokes.

- Use the same exercise as above but now in the cross-court. This exercise is a good practice for doubles play.

- Play two shots cross-court and two shots down the line. One player stays on one side.

- Use the same exercise with both players recovering to the middle of the court after each shot.

- Use the same exercise as above with two shots cross and one down the line. The change of direction will speed up this way.

- Use the same exercise as above with one shot down the line and one down the line.

- Play two shots cross-court and one down the line. Once you play down the line, it is up to the other player to start the sequence again with the cross-court rally.

- Start the point by feeding the ball wide cross-court to the player on the other side of the net, starting at the single line, and play out the point.

- Play points with two players playing against one player.

Caroline Wozniacki

PROGRESSION OF BEGINNING TENNIS PLAYERS

There is a preparation phase before young kids start playing tennis. In Europe, the kids start with indoor training, the winter before they start playing outside. They practice with mini tennis. The kids experiment with different size balls with bouncing the ball, throwing the ball, and hitting with wooden paddles.

1. **Quick Start tennis** is a great way to get the kids started in teaching them the basics of tennis. The nets are smaller and lower, the balls are made from foam to keep the bounce lower, and the rackets are lighter. This particular method of introducing tennis to kids makes it easy to learn and fun to play.

2. **Mini tennis** is the next phase, with the courts just a little larger than Quick Start. The balls are made for mini tennis and the rackets fit the student's size. The balls look like regular tennis balls but are actually much softer, so they bounce low with less speed. Feed the ball to the first player and instead of having them hit the ball to the opponent, ask them to bounce the ball up in the air once at contact point before returning it to the opponent. The opponent will then repeat the same action before returning it to the first player.

3. **Mini tennis with patterns** teaches the students to play a predetermined pattern that will help them change direction to the ball with consistency. Patterns teach the kids to maneuver the opponent around the court. This will help them recognize the weaknesses of the opponents and how to exploit them.

4. **Mini tennis with points** is the next exercise in having players compete and improve their competitive and mental skills. Playing points will train students to enjoy practice, competition, and the game of tennis.

5. **Preparation tennis** is the first real lesson the students have on an actual tennis court with tennis balls. This is the time to introduce them to the forehand and backhand grips. The western grip and eastern backhand

grip are recommended for young players (see grips). Have the students try bouncing the ball down toward the ground with their racket and then upward in the air to get a feel for the ball. Players who started with Quick Start or played mini tennis may have some basic skills already.

6. **Playing with low-pressure balls** on a regular court is a good transition to familiarize them with the size of the court. The lower bounce of the low-pressure balls assists them in using the correct grips. Avoid using regular balls too soon. They bounce too high in relation to the size of a young player, which can cause the students to change their grips.

7. **Introduction of the forehand grip and stroke** to beginning players is often introduced with five points: the grip, the stance, the backswing, the contact point, and the follow through. By keeping it simple, your students will understand the topics better and learn faster. One player can stop the ball at contact point and play it back after the bounce while the other player can play it back directly with the full and complete forehand stroke. By alternating this drill, students can practice the contact point and control of the ball by reducing the speed.

8. **Introduction of the backhand grip and stroke** is usually more complicated. Most young players use two hands to hit the backhand. This takes more coordination and better footwork to hit the ball. They do, however, have more power to control the racket. By teaching them how to grip both hands on the racket, you can solve a lot of problems. Keeping both elbows loose creates a smooth stroke. Repeat the same exercise as with the forehand.

9. **The service stroke** is the most coordinative action to master. With both arms and hands performing different actions, it can confuse the student in the beginning. Introduce the serve in separate parts. Practice the toss first. Then toss the ball in coordination with the backswing. The toss arm and backswing form the letter *Y* at the top of the backswing. Practice hitting the ball with the racket in the ready position, between the shoulders, before trying the whole motion all together.

10. **Forehand strokes with movement** are easiest to practice with the coach feeding the students three balls each along the baseline. The players have to seek the proper stance and the right distance to the ball.

The goal is to hit as many balls to the target as they can and to keep a balanced position during contact. Your students will receive a lot of balls when rotating them around over the baseline.

11. **Backhand stroke with movement** is the same as the previous drill. The coach can control the speed, direction, and difficulty of the feed in maintaining the confidence of the players at all time. The goal is to improve consistency during movement.

12. **Match play tryouts** are necessary to give the students experience in competition and a purpose for practicing. Keep the games simple to give them the highest chance of early success. Confidence will make them try harder in practice.

13. **Consistency with forehand and backhand** is where technical and tactical aspects start to overlap. Explain how technical aspects can improve consistency; early preparation of racket and feet, contact point in front, and the trajectory over the net all assist in improving consistency. It also connects with the general strategy and tactics in specifics. Practicing consistency with juniors can become a competitive game by having them try to hit the ball, back and forth, as often as possible.

14. **Directing the serve** by hitting the targets in the service box is the first objective. Learning to hit to the weaker side from the opponent is a secondary objective. Find the targets from large to small. Let students compete to see who can do this the best. Show them the tactical advantages by playing some points connected to target areas and the possible returns of the opponent.

15. **Depth of the strokes** helps the students realize the size of the court and how to pressure the opponent. You can assist them with visualizing a higher net or having them hit the ball beyond the service line. After sufficient practice, try the same in a game to enhance their strategy and consistency.

16. **Change of direction** can be challenging at first. Practice down the line and cross-court separately before combining a pattern. By introducing a pre-arranged pattern the students will have more confidence and you

can see if they are able to perform the pattern as instructed. A good pattern to start with is: two strokes cross-court and two strokes down the line. One player stays on one side while the other moves to recover the balls back to one half of the court.

17. **Match play** is the test to how your students are progressing. It is an excellent way to see what they have picked up and where they still need some attention and practice.

Maria Sharapova

Martin van Daalen

TEACHING EQUIPMENT

Court Attributes

There are several attributes and props you can use in creating targets or fields for practice. It provides players with a visual aid in aiming and executing certain strokes. Coaches and players should use these props as much as possible in their training. You can assign a target area by using cones or flat plastic mats. Another option on hard courts is to use colored tape to mark an area. Some other methods, for coaches to consider, are the use of lines or targets areas over the net. There are several companies where you can buy these online (see web pages).

Ball Machines

These devices have some purpose in practice but are quite expensive for the amount of time they are used. A ball machine can be a good tool to practice consistency. I used it myself to train when I did not have anyone around to hit balls with. I would set up repetitive patterns on the machine in order to simulate a rally. I think it has its use at times, but not in continuous use. With more advanced players, it can be used to perfect a certain technique or pattern. There are many different models available from different companies with a wide price range. The possibilities range from speed, height, and direction to spin and feeding frequency. For beginners, I would recommend a simple and less expensive model for feeding easy low-speed balls without spin and moderate height as to give them opportunity for more repetition and consistency.

Backboard or Wall

Whenever you read a book from a former top player, it will not escape your attention how most players mention how relentless they were in hitting balls against a backboard or a wall. Another interesting point is that they always seemed to do this on their own. The passion for the game and the willpower to succeed definitely played a big role in all of these players.

Formerly, it was used more frequently, and I was no exception. I remember doing this myself for hours when I did not have anyone to play with at the club. I realized how much it helped me to focus and concentrate and made me more consistent and physically stronger. With a tennis wall, you never have to worry about the ball coming back—it always does! You would find me there every day since I was the first to get there in the afternoon. Playing on the backboard made me think of different ways to practice, and I even got the groundskeeper to paint lines on the wall for me to aim at.

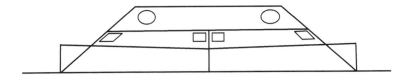

An example of a tennis wall or backboard in
perspective with target areas

I have seen many backboards and tennis walls at clubs all over the world, but I rarely see kids practicing on them anymore. This could be due to the impact of computer games and cell phones on our society. Many kids find it difficult to focus and have a hard time concentrating over long periods of time. Even so, I think it is important for coaches to teach players how to practice on the wall and use it to their advantage. Teaching kids how to do this properly or what games they can play can stimulate them the practice there more often. It will help in developing better tennis players.

You can practice the following:

- **Baseline Strokes**
  You can practice the depth of the strokes by playing in the upper box displayed in the picture. Practice left to right by moving the ball around above the net.

- **Volleys**
  By standing closer to the wall, you can volley the ball back on the wall and play left and right to alternate strokes.

Martin van Daalen

- **Service**
  You can practice the targeting of the serve by aiming in the service boxes as they are portrayed in perspective on the backboard.

- **Combination Rallies**
  Play a rally using all the strokes. Start with the serve, hit some rallies, approach on a shorter ball, and move in to hit some volleys.

Video and Instruction Films

The use of video as an instruction tool is very valuable to players with visual learning. Showing them how they performed gives them a realistic feedback on their strokes and movement on the court. Video is excellent in detecting technical errors or fixing a stroke. It should also be used to build confidence in the player by confirming their performance. Try to use video analysis sparingly to keep the interest of the player high. Too much analysis can be distracting and makes the players too critical of their own development. Instruction videos can be very valuable in stimulating the students to greater improvement and passion for the game.

Training Notebook

A notebook is a valuable possession for any player to keep the details of their improvements and results. Making notes of what has worked or what needs to be improved can be very helpful. The players can always look back at their notes as a reference of training. It is also a possible feedback for the coach of what the students learned in practice and what they retained in their memory. There have been many great players that used this method of recording notes for themselves about practice or about their opponents. Ivan Lendl used to keep a record of each player he played and added notes each time he played the same opponent. Keeping a notebook has proven to be a successful tool in the development of many players and it will work for you too!

TRAINING AND TOURNAMENT PLAN

Before a coach can start working with a player, an analysis needs to be made of development of the player's game. To make a plan, the coach needs to acquire the following information:

- **Age**
  In order to make a lesson plan, you need to know the age of the student(s) you are working with. You would not teach the same lesson to an eight-year-old as to a fourteen-year-old. The subject matter needs to be appropriate to the age and skill level of each player.

- **Gender**
  The subject matter is mostly the same with gender differences. This might change as the players become more proficient (see *Teaching Advanced Players*). In teaching boys and girls, the coach needs a different approach and attitude to communicate. In teaching boys, the coach can be much more direct in corrections and feedback after matches. With girls, you have to be aware that corrections are often taken personally. In general, the coach should start every correction with a positive comment before moving on to a correction. With girls, this is a crucial step in communicating information.

- **Playing Experience**
  The skill level and match experience of a player are important factors to consider before organizing a lesson plan. As a coach, you do not want to jump ahead too far and introduce material that the players are not equipped to execute. On the other hand, if the subject matter is too easy, the students will become bored and may not try as hard. The key is to find the proper subject level and subjects to keep them highly interested and motivated to improve.

- **Strengths and Weaknesses Analysis**
  The optimal way to train your students is by incorporating subjects from the analysis you made that will help them improve their skills. A good coach will spend more time on weaknesses that need improvement

while maintaining or strengthening the weapons in a player's game. The key is to organize this all in a training plan that has a progression of new subjects and a repetition and improvement of old subjects.

- **Activity**
  The progression and intensity of a training plan depends on the subject matter and improvements in prior lessons. The coach has to analyze the intensity of the training and the improvements of the students. The intensity of the training can be measured in quantity or the level of intensity of the performance. If necessary, adjustments can be made to the training plan in intensity and subject matter.

- **Intensity**
  The intensity and subject matter needs to be coordinated with the tournaments and/or competition of the student. Close to competition, the intensity of the lessons might be higher, but the duration will be shorter. The training will be focused on strategy and mental preparation rather than technical issues.

- **Goals of the Student**
  It is important to know what goals your students have set for themselves. These goals can be performance goals, ranking goals, or outcome goals. Performance goals can be to improve certain strokes or the execution of a strategy. Ranking goals are solely focused in reaching a certain ranking in a specific time period. Outcome goals are the results in matches or tournaments. The coach needs to investigate what those goals are and discuss them with the player prior to making a training and tournament plan.

After considering all this information, it is possible to make an extensive training and tournament plan. This can be a semi-annual or annual training plan, but personally, I have always preferred a plan for the whole year; most students are motivated by knowing their development plan for the future. Development plans become more important when teaching intermediate and advanced players.

Training Plan

- **Goals** (long-term and short-term)
  To make a training plan, you have to create short- and long-term-goals. These goals will help determine the subjects you will teach, when to train, and the intensity of the training.

  The *short-term goals* should be objectives set by the player, parents, and coach for improving subjects of immediate importance and/or relative ease in learning. Example: change contact point and follow through.

  The *long-term goals* should be objectives set by the player, parents, and coach for improving subjects of long-term development and/ or difficult nature in learning. Example: learning serve and volley game and strategy.

- **Corrections** (and how to go about them)
  Make a list of subjects that need correction and a plan on how to correct them. It is not always easy to determine what needs to be corrected. Some technical issues can be hidden and are not always easy to detect with the naked eye. Taking some video of your student and using slow motion can be a very helpful tool.

  In the coaches' education courses I have followed and in the many instructional tennis books I have read, one of the things lacking is a "how to fix" section. So I have included a chapter on how to correct certain problems in teaching (see chapters "Technical Instruction" and "Problem Solving").

- **Periodization Plan** (planning what to train and when)
  This should be a detailed plan of what to train on which day and/or week. A plan is needed to help the coach avoid a haphazard approach and zigzagging through the development of the player. Having a logical order in training strokes, physical training, and tactical and mental development helps accelerate the learning process. The objective is to utilize a plan that is well-balanced, with a good mix of topics that meet the physical demands of each player.

Martin van Daalen

Periodization Plan

Day	Tournament	Training content	Technical	Tactical	Physical	Mental
1	-	Ground strokes		Depth		
2	-	Service	Contact	Targets		
3	Local			Consistency		Strategy
4	Local			Consistency		Strategy
5	-	Volley	Footwork		Speed	
6	-	Return		Targets		
7	Super series			Approach		

By using a periodization plan, you are able to carefully plan what topics to use for the player (or groups of players) for the weeks they are training and for the days when they are playing tournaments or competition.

Above is an example of how you could coordinate the training with tournament play. This will help achieve better results in tournaments as well as motivate the students to a more productive practice.

Note: Just before competition, the focus should be on tactical and mental training. This is not a good time to make technical corrections or introduce new techniques. You want the player to think about the strategy of the game during competition. During competition, you don't want the player to think about how to hit the ball, but more on where to hit the ball!

To practice without a plan is like taking a journey without a map; you might have a lot of detours and get lost along the way.

Tournament Plan

In making a competition or tournament plan, be sure to include the following

- Performance goals
  These should include subjects such as improving the strokes, strategy or tactics, physical improvements, or the consistency of execution. Goals will increase the purpose of competition.

- Outcome goals
  These could be about trying to win a match or a certain tournament. Later on, this can change to participating in a certain tournament through ranking or maybe even a ranking goal.

- Detailed tournament schedule
  The schedule should to be a semi-annual or annual plan that includes all the tournaments throughout the tennis season so you can make adjustments when necessary.

Scheduling

The scheduling of tournaments needs to be well thought out, with the development of the student in mind. *Don't play tournaments until the player is comfortable playing practice matches first.* Start with a few novice tournaments and then, if necessary, correct the errors during practice. The goal should always be to try and win several matches in a row. This enhances the confidence and desire to train and work harder.

Quantity

The number of tournaments is related to the level of play. As a rookie player, students should try to play ten to fifteen tournaments a year. A junior player should compete in ten to twenty-five tournaments a year. This number also depends on how well they are playing (number of matches) and the technical development of the player. Try to play two or three tournaments in a row to acquire a rhythm of play.

Level

There are several different levels of tournaments in each age group ranging from novice tournaments in the districts and sections to national and international events.

A good rule of thumb in playing events is to never move on to the next level until you have mastered or are dominating the level you are competing in.

A win-loss ratio to keep in mind is at least two wins to one loss, but a three to one ratio would be more preferable in order to keep confidence high. (This is very important when working with juniors) With intermediate and advanced players, it is possible to play three different competition levels: (1) tournaments to win, (2) tournaments they are competitive in reaching at least the quarter final, and (3) events to play up a level for experience.

Tournaments

There are many events to choose in each district and section of the country. Some different types of tournaments are the following:

1. Sectional   Junior and adult events
2. National   Junior and adult events
3. International   Junior ETA (European Tennis Association)
                                      Junior ITF (International Tennis Federation)
                                      Pro events (ITF, ATP, WTA)

District and Section

- Junior events: - Age group events
(ten through eighteen years of age)
(Local to designated to sectional events
Entry by ranking or standing
There are also rookie events available
You can play up until your birthday in that month)

- Adult events: - Age group events by level of play
- League tennis by level of play

- Open events: - Prize and/or money events
                    Anybody can enter

National Events:

- Junior events: - Age group events (ten through
                        eighteen years of age)
                        (entry by ranking or standing)
                    - National open's are regional entry events
                    - Nationals or super national are tournaments
                        (spring, clay, hard, and winter championships)

- Adult events: - Age group events by level of play

International Events:

- Junior events: - ITF junior events (age thirteen to eighteen)
                    - ETA junior events (ages twelve, fourteen,
                        and sixteen)

- Pro events: - ITF events (futures and challengers)
                - ATP and WTA events

Martin van Daalen

Junior Tournament Development Track

As a junior, it is wise to go from the level where you can win matches to the next level and so on. For parents, coaches, and players this is what a normal development track would look like:

Players who are eight to ten years of age could begin competing in *rookie* events. They need to win some matches in each level before moving to the next.

If your student is very competitive, they can move from playing sectional events to nationals by acquiring enough ranking points.

There are usually several different ways to qualify for national events. Most countries use a system where your ranking will qualify your entry. Another possibility is to qualify with a regional event.

Most countries will organize national events throughout the year with the national championship in summer and winter. In the United States, there four major national events:

- Easter bowl
- Clay courts
- Hard courts
- Winter championships

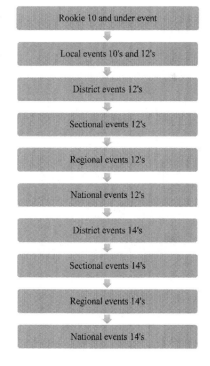

If your student keeps winning matches in each of these events, it becomes time for them to try playing in the next age group level (see chart above). Confidence is the most important mental factor in stimulating your student to feel accomplishments with a willingness to improve. To harness this, it is essential to give them an opportunity to succeed and not play up too soon! As player progress, they are able to play a mix of events in different age groups and levels.

Tournament Plan

Name:

Age:

Week	Local	National	Events	Total
1			Local	5
2			National	3
3	Local			
4	Super Series			
5				
7		Regional		
8				
9		National Open		
10				
11				
12	Designated			
13				
14				
15				
16	Local			
17				
18				
19	Designated			
20				
21				
22		Spring Tournament		

By creating an individual tournament plan for each player, you are able to plan and coordinate your lessons much more accurately to the needs of the student. Choose tournaments where the player can be successful. Make sure they don't play too many or too few events. When making a plan, keep track of the type of events and how many you are planning semi-annually or annually (see tournament plan) This way, you can plan how much they play and when to take a break. Keeping the goals of the player and coach in mind, choose the tournaments the player would like to enter by ranking or by qualifying into the tournaments in the future. In order to schedule a plan, you have to work backward from that point to ensure entry and to achieve your goal.

Tournaments should be a fun and social event with a competitive spirit.

Playing Tournaments

To play tournaments, you need information on how to enter, where to go, and what time you need to be there. This information is freely available and located on specific websites from the tournaments. You will need the information listed below to get started.

Fact sheet information is a fact sheet page, listed on the web, with all the pertinent information from the tournament concerning dates, entry information, hotels, or other accommodations with directions to hotel and tournament site. You can find this fact sheet on the websites from the appropriate organizations (see info and web pages).

Membership of a federation is usually required for a membership number for entry into tournaments. You can find membership information on each country's official federation website. For example, most U.S. tournaments require a USTA membership.

Ranking is a list that ranks players according to their results. It is also used to obtain entry into the events. The ranking can be different in each country but is usually some form of point system. For each round, you win you receive points. You should educate yourself on how the ranking works to properly advise your student. You can find specific instruction on the federation website (see info and web pages).

Entry into the junior events is usually submitted online. For entry in events, you will most likely need to acquire a federation membership. After you have completed the entry, you should receive confirmation by the event. If you do not receive this receipt, contact the tournament director! After entry, you can look up the entry list to see who has entered.

The **entry list** is the list of players that have entered for the event. The list will be posted as soon as the entry date has passed. You can find these lists on the same website as the tournament.

The **draw** is the tournament list of players who are matched up to play one another. A draw is made up of seeded players and unseeded players. Seeded players receive certain spots in the draw through ranking. You should make yourself familiar with the proceedings in making a draw. This will help you to understand the tournament play in general and ensure no mistakes are made.

The **acceptance list** is the list of players that have been accepted to the tournament. This list is usually generated by rankings from the players.

The **cutoff** is the number from a ranking of the last player to be accepted to the event. Knowing the last ranking number to be accepted will give you an indication of the strength of the event.

Coaching at Tournaments

The coaching of players during tournaments is quite different from teaching them at home or at the club. The pressure of playing a match (whether you know your opponent or not) with coaches and parents watching can add to the anxiety and excitement of the player. When preparing a player for tournament play, a coach will focus on the technical and physical aspects first. As the tournament approaches, the focus will shift from technical and physical aspects to tactical and mental aspects. All coaches will make some mistakes along the way, but here are some tips to help avoid some of the most common ones:

Make It Fun

Playing matches and tournaments should always be fun! This is a very important concept for coaches and parents to remember. Most young children enjoy being in an environment where they can play with other children. At this age, though everyone enjoys winning, they are more interested in just playing the game and having fun. In competition, it is possible for players, coaches, and parents to get carried away with their emotions. It is the duty and responsibility of the coach to ensure that everyone keeps their emotions and attitudes in check. Kids learn from the examples of adults. If any of these problems arise, remind parents that best results are achieved with positive reinforcement and by praising players for their accomplishments.

Preparation

Players need to understand how to prepare for competition. It does not start on the day of competition but in the practice leading up to the competition. The practice will have much more purpose when there is a goal to work for. The other part of the preparation is learning what to bring to the match and to have a prematch routine. Kids will not be used to packing their bags with extra clothing, a track suit or coat, a towel, food, and drinks. The prematch routine consists of a physical warm-up, warming up on the court, and discussing a game plan. Teaching players to perform this routine before each match will instill a discipline that enhances their performance.

Pre-match Coaching

Beginning players don't need to be overloaded with information. Teach them that enjoying the competition is just as important as knowing how to play the game. Coaching them above their skill level, by stressing the winning or expectations, will result in a heightened anxiety level. This will show in acting out on court and attitude problems. The game plan should be short and to the point. Refrain from using long drawn-out speeches and difficult scenarios. Focus the players on simple strategies that are easy to understand and execute.

On-Court Coaching

Coaching players on court, during match play, is a valuable tool in their mental and tactical development. The purpose of on-court coaching is to teach the player how to "think" their way through a match. It is not to try to influence the outcome of the match. Keep in mind that on-court coaching is restricted in certain matches. In this case, avoid talking to the players during matches. Team matches are ideal to use for on-court coaching in playing league tennis. Team tennis is very popular in Europe and is regarded by most to be the pinnacle event of the year. It is very much an accepted form of coaching there and coaches are providing instruction on the change over. When coaching on the court, try to avoid giving too much information because it confuses the player. Coaching players during matches where on-court coaching is not allowed will take their attention from *inside* the court to *outside* the court. They will often experience a breakdown or inconsistency in strategy and lose confidence. The result is that the player will constantly be looking for support from outside the court instead of seeking the answers from within. Tennis requires the players to quickly adapt to situations on the court. Coaches that establish this type of relationship with their players will experience difficulty in teaching independent thinking, problem solving, and building the confidence of the player.

Post-match Coaching

Debriefing players on their performance after the match is a delicate matter. As a coach, it takes some patience and diplomacy to navigate yourself through this potential minefield. The first thing to consider is the emotions of the player, not your own feelings as a coach or parent. Directly after the match, encourage the player and then give them time to cool down. Most players are emotional after they complete a match and will not be able to process information given to them at this time. Allow them time to think through the details of the match, what they did well, and where they need to improve. As a coach or a parent, you may be emotional after the match as well. This can affect what you say and how your message is delivered to the player. Take your time and don't comment right away after the match.

Guidelines to post-match discussions:

1. Let the player speak first about their match.
2. Try not to interrupt so they don't get distracted or frustrated.
3. Give your opinion on their assessment.
4. Give your own opinion on the match.
5. Let them have some final comments.
6. Make a recap and list of what to work on.

Martin van Daalen

Note: As the players progress and become more experienced players, they might want to write some notes down. The notes can include as follows:

- Match information: date, opponent, score, etc.
- Strengths and weaknesses of the opponent
- Notes on the match: what went well, what did not go well
- Conclusions

If a player writes notes on the performance of the match, they will become much more specific with their observations instead of saying nonspecific things like: "My forehand was not working well today." This is where the coach can step in and do the real postmatch coaching. Be patient and ask for explanations.

TEACHING TACTICAL ASPECTS OF THE GAME

The tactical development of the player has to go hand in hand with the technical, physical, and mental development. It is important for the player to understand how these four pillars are interwoven with one another. The tactical development can be taught, but I have seen players who have a knack of figuring this out for themselves. You could call them tactically-talented tennis players. There are many tactical aspects to teach, but I will stick to the basics for beginning and intermediate players in this book.

Strategy in Playing Tennis

The basic concept of strategy is to optimally use your strengths by exploiting the weaknesses of your opponent. You have to devise specific tactics to do this well.

Tactical Situation: Singles—Doubles

1. Baseline play
2. Service and return   (for beginning players)
3. Net play

4. Transition   (for intermediate and
5. Playing against the net player   advanced players)

Baseline Play
As a beginning player, you can learn to exploit the weaknesses of your opponent by using some very simple methods.

1. **Consistency** is the first tactic every player should use as a game plan to combat an opponent. Consistency is the first element to break down when a player becomes nervous. In playing longer rallies, with the ball going back and forth, the pressure builds up and mistakes might follow. Consistency is often used as a weapon at any level of play, but even more so in junior tennis.

Practice: Hit many balls in a row. At first, hit the ball up the middle of the court, then cross-court both ways. Once the player has mastered that skill, try different patterns with combinations of down the line and cross-court.

2. **Depth** is not only a different way to force a mistake from your opponent but is also an accomplishment of four important factors in defending yourself. It provides you with extra time with a longer ball flight. It also assists you in covering the court more easily, with the opponent having fewer angles available. It often generates short balls from the opponent with the opportunity to attack and use the wider angles against them (see picture below). And finally, better depth generates opportunities to move the general position of a player closer to the baseline. This is a good position for defense and offense.

Note: As the player becomes more experienced, the change of depth of the ground strokes becomes another factor in disrupting the positioning of the player. This enables them to outmaneuver their opponent and draw mistakes.

Practice: To practice depth, place targets on the court and/or raise the height of the net to change the trajectory. An easy way to do this is by placing a net pole under the center of the net.

3. **Change of direction** is the next progression in developing tactical skills. As a beginning player, it is important to understand that playing the ball back in the direction it came from has the highest probability of success. Changing direction takes some time to learn. Understanding when to make this shot choice is the key. It becomes a higher percentage shot when the ball is inside the sideline, slower in pace and spin, and less deep in the court.

Practice: Have player A stay on one side and player B plays back to that side. Have them practice two shots cross-court and two shots down the line. After mastering this drill, try this again but now finding the right moment to hit down the line. You can perform the same drill with points. It will improve the strategy and competitive spirit.

Service and Return

These tactical aspects of the game are the starting points of the rally for each player. There are some basic strategies to the serve and return:

1. Consistency - Getting the ball in the court is the first objective
2. Depth   - Used to neutralize the opponent
3. Weaker side - To draw mistakes or weak returns from the opponent

These basic strategies are listed in order of importance to a player's shot choice in relation to the difficulty factor of the tactical situation. The player only has a short time before the point and during the execution to make a decision to weigh the risk and reward chances.

Service

The serve is the most coordinated stroke for a tennis player to perform. It is also one of the first strokes to break down under pressure. Putting sufficient time into practicing consistency and targeting is important for all players. Practice both first and second serves. In fact, it becomes more important to practice the second serve than to practice the first serve. A player that can trust their second serve to hold up under pressure will be more confident and relaxed and hit the first serve with less fear of missing. A dominant first serve will be the result (Pete Sampras is a good example of becoming so confident with his serves that he often hit two first serves).

Note: Make sure, when practicing the service action, to not exceed more than twenty minutes due to increased chances of injuries. It is better to have three sessions of ten minutes than thirty minutes at one time. Also, practice the body serves (aimed directly at the body). It is difficult for any players to return body serves, but even more so for less experienced players!

Martin van Daalen

Practice: Progression is important to gaining confidence in execution. With this in mind, practice the easy targets first before moving on to the difficult ones. The picture shows the target area in the service boxes.

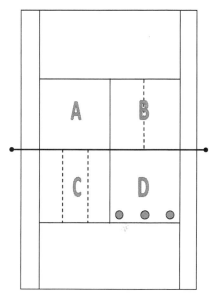

A - Whole service box

B - Half the service box

C - One-third of the box

D - Specific targets

Make specific goals in hitting the targets a certain number of times to practice the consistency, before moving on to the following progression in development. Practice both first and second serves.

The Return

The basic strategy for the return is very similar to the strategy of the serve. However, the tactical objectives (1 and 2) are different in returning a first serve and a second serve.

- First serve: 1 Defensive (getting the ball back)
  2 Neutralizing (depth and target)

Returning the first serve should always have the objective to get the ball back in the court no matter what. When possible, the second objective should be depth and a target area to neutralize or exploit the opponent. For the beginning tennis player, it pays to play the return back to the middle of the court. This is the largest target area and ensures a high percentage return. The opponent has fewer angles to attack.

- Second serve: 1 Neutralizing (depth and target)
  2 Offensive (target and pace)

Returning the second serve can be more aggressive in nature as long as consistency is maintained. The second serve will generally have less pace, resulting in more initiative possibility of the returning player.

For beginning tennis players, these are the three basic target return areas:

- Backhand

- Center

- Forehand

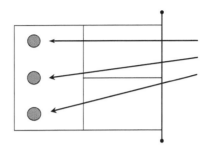

Practice the return from both first and second serve and return to these basic target areas. Make it a goal to return a certain number of balls to each target area.

Net Play

The basic net play strategy is to finish off the points at the net. Closing the distance between a player and an opponent will shorten the reaction time. At the net position, you can obtain a greater angle of attack to finish the point before the opponent can run the ball down. Here are some tactical instructions for beginners:

- *Closing the net* is the first step in the learning process. Players have to learn to move their feet first in making a volley. The closer they can get to the net, the higher percentage chance they will have with a volley. The closer net position will create more angles in hitting the ball downward and sideways (see picture below).

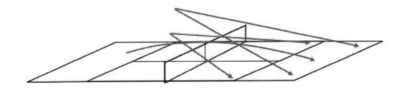

Martin van Daalen

- *Keep the execution simple.* Don't try to make it too fancy. By flexing the wrist backward and keeping the backswing short, the player will be able to step forward and keep the racket more stable at contact.

- *Aim for the open court.* This is the first thought the player should have in mind. Fewer options make the execution of the stroke easier. As the player becomes more proficient, they can learn other options.

- *Hitting the overhead like the service action* is a good way to teach this specialty shot to beginning players. It will be a transition of this particular stroke before they learn the specifics of the overhead.

Practice: Doubles is a fun way to introduce net play to beginning players. You can side step all the transition shots, for a moment, and still have them enjoy this part of the game.

Teaching a Game Plan

In preparation for competition, you have to teach players to think strategically and tactically to play against their opponent. The game plan is constructed from several components:

1-Information about the opponent   (strength and weaknesses)
2-The surface they are playing on   (play style)
3-The weather conditions   (preparation)

The strengths and weaknesses of the opponent is the most important information needed to make a game plan. It dictates how to play against your opponent and to prevent them from finding your weaknesses. The knowledge of the student's capabilities to execute the game plan should fit to the comfort level of the player. Teach them to make a game plan to outmaneuver the opponent by reducing their capabilities (neutralizing) and enhancing the possibilities to attack. The strategy here should be a three-part plan that consists of the following:

1. Where to serve and start the rally
2. How to return and start the rally
3. How to finish the rally in patterns

Note: It will help to make a list of strengths and weaknesses from both the opponent and the player. This makes it very clear what strategy/tactic to play. This is especially true if your player is a visual learner. It pays to write the game plan and even draw the patterns of play.

The surface is important in determining the type of shots and patterns needed to play the proper strategy. Playing on a clay court is different, in style, than a hard court. The footwork and movement will influence the physical capabilities and strategy.

The weather conditions can change the way you play. The wind and heat index have a big influence on the capabilities of play. Playing in windy conditions requires an adjustment of the footwork, shot choice, and target area. The feet need to be in motion all the time to adjust to sudden direction changes of the ball. The shot choices need to be more conservative with larger target areas for higher percentage play in the wind. The heat index (the combination of temperature and humidity) will determine your preparation in bringing more fluids to the court and taking as much time as possible in between points. It mostly affects the intensity of play and endurance becomes a factor in combating your opponent.

Martin van Daalen

Teaching the Basics of Doubles

Playing doubles requires a lot of skill from the players. With the players already in place at the net, the speed of the game increases and the target areas of the return are reduced in size and direction. With the rallies becoming shorter, the consistency and accuracy have to increase to be successful in doubles. Being creative and flexible under pressure are important intangibles to develop as a doubles player. Here are some of the most important topics for practicing doubles:

* **Positioning**
  The positioning of players in doubles is the starting position, on the court, before play has commenced. The positioning is an important signal to your partner and the opponents of possible strategies. The positions of the players in the service games are different from the return games (see picture below).

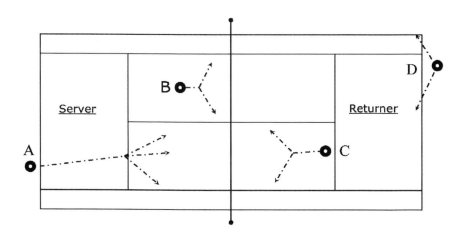

Player A serves from the middle of their side of the court. This position varies from the singles position in order to cover that half of the court. The player can either stay in that position to play baseline stroke (beginning players) or move in after the serve and play the volley (intermediate and advanced players)

Player B takes the net position in the middle of the service box and moves in as the ball from the server passes by. The net player covers half the court from this position and assists the approaching player in covering the middle of the court from the return.

Player C watches the movements of player B to intercept the return. Player C moves in to cover the net if player B does not try to intercept (poach) and volley the ball.

Player D returns the serve and reacts to the exchange of the rally from the players at the net. If his partner, player C, moves across to intercept the volley, player D might have to switch over to the other side to cover the court.

- **Serve and Return for Doubles**
  These two strokes start the rally every point of the match with either serving or returning. They fit excellently together in training both at the same time. When serving, practice consistency and direction to the forehand, the backhand, and the body targets. You can use cones in the service box to improve the accuracy and consistency or use tape to mark an area. When returning, players can practice this by using the single lines as targets. They can hit the ball cross-court or down the line. You can also introduce the lob over the net player. This is specifically used on the return in doubles play. A very efficient way to practice doubles is to have all four players play cross-court points simultaneously.

  Teaching the tactics of the serve and return for doubles involves the relation between the targets and the possible returns with the actions of the players. All the targets have different possibilities. Walk your players through the plays as they unfold so they have a better understanding how to play the game.

- **Net Play**
  Players are much more frequent at the net in doubles than singles and therefore need to practice this part of the game more often. There are two types of net play to practice for this level:

  1. *Playing at the net*
     This involves the role of the two players at the net and how they play their part in the doubles strategy. Running across the net and

Martin van Daalen

cutting off the volley, also called poaching, is an important part of practice for both players. Learning how and when to do this is the key to good net play. The timing of the movement needs to be coordinated with the serve and the return from the opponent. The net player can either communicate this action with their partner beforehand or decide at the last moment when seeing the possibility of interception.

2. *Approaching the net*
   The player moves to the net from a short return from the opponent or behind the serve and volley as a server. You can feed the short return into play and play out the point or have the players play serve and volley in the cross-courts. The main concept to teach for the volley is to play cross-court when the volley is low and to hit at the net player when the return is high.

- **Playing against the Net Players**
  This part of the game needs more practice than it usually receives. The speed of the rally exchange increases between net player and baseline player. Teach the baseline players to keep four targets in mind: two body targets, the ball through the middle in between the net players, and the lob. The angle shots are a temptation to play but often result in a short drop volley that is even harder to return. Understanding the basic strategies for doubles and keeping it simple by explaining how the points will unfold increases the enjoyment in accomplishment of play.

TEACHING INTERMEDIATE PLAYERS

After some years of experience, the players are ready for the next learning phase. This involves the details of the strokes and the physical and mental game. When teaching more specific parts of the tennis game, keep in mind to use subjects from all tactical situations and progression in learning:

Tactical Situations	Progression of Learning
1. Baseline play	1. Consistency
2. Serve and return	2. Depth
3. Approaching the net	3. Direction
4. Net play	4. Spin
5. Playing against the net player	5. Power
	6. Tempo of play

Spin, power, and tempo of play will come in to play later when the student has more experience. Spin might become a factor in playing the game but should not be a topic of learning for beginning tennis players.

Subjects for Baseline Play

- **How to win cross-court rallies** by using consistency and depth in the cross-court. By pushing the opponent wider and deeper behind the baseline and playing consistent, the opponent might become nervous and try to hit the ball down the line at the wrong time and draw an error.

- **How to defend yourself** by hitting the ball back to the center of the court. By hitting the ball higher over the net and deeper in the court, you enhance the chances of defending yourself by reducing the angles for the opponent to attack.

- **How to use the open court** and keep your opponent on the run. The pressure increases on the opponent when keeping them on the run. They might try for too much and will create errors or short returns from your opponent.

Martin van Daalen

- **How to open the court** and pressure the weakness of the opponent. This is accomplished by playing deep and wide to the strength first before attacking the weaker side of the opponent, who now has to hit this shot under pressure.

- **How to open the court by playing down the line.** After establishing the cross-court rally, the opponent will hang more in the corner and leave the down the line open. Choosing the right time to hit this shot, when the ball is shorter and inside the sideline, is a requirement for success. Play with a margin for error; the depth of the ball is more important than hitting close to the sideline.

- **How to wrong-foot your opponent** by playing back and forth to the corners and then doubling back and hitting it to the same corner. Your opponent might react too late and lose balance during the rally or reach the shot too late to control it.

Subjects for Serve and Return Play

- **How to open the court** by serving wide and opening the court. With a wide serve, the opponent will be forced out of position. This will open up the court with the possibility to attack and move in behind to finish the point.

- **How to use body shots** to draw an error or weak return. The opponent will often not expect the body shot and/or react too late for a proper return. This often causes the return to fall short in the court for an offensive position.

- **How to neutralize your opponent** by returning the ball high and deep through the middle of the court. The height and depth of the ball will force the opponent in a defensive position deep behind the baseline with fewer angles to attack.

- **How to take initiative with the return.** By playing to the weaker baseline stroke from your opponent, it is very likely to receive a short or weak response.

- **How to take initiative with the return.** By stepping forward and attacking the second serve, you will pressure the opponent by rushing them in hitting the responding baseline stroke or drawing service errors.

Subjects for Approaching the Net

- **Why hit the approach shot down the line.** By playing the ball straight in front and not cross-court, you can reach and cover the net angles more easily. Hitting to a big target down the line reduces the cross-court angle and enhances consistency.

- **How to open the court on a cross-court approach.** If the opponent is moved off the court with an angle shot and returns the ball short down the line or the middle, it will pay off to approach the ball cross-court to the open court.

Subjects for Net Play

- **How to close the net.** By stepping in and getting closer to the net, the player can find more angles to play the volley sideways and shorter in the court.

- **How to hit overheads with consistency.** By choosing a big target to the open court, fewer mistakes will be made on overheads and increase the consistency.

- **How to intercept a volley at the net in doubles.** By moving across the net when the opponent hits the ball it is possible to cut off the volley (poach) at the net and place the volley in between the opponents for a winner.

Subjects for Playing against the Net Player

- **How to pass the net player.** By hitting low cross-court, the net player is moved out of position with less opportunity to hit a winner. It will either result in a pass, or the difficult volley will set up the pass on the next shot.

- **How to pass the opponent with the lob.** A low return shot will draw the opponent closer to the net, followed by a lob over their head. Try to aim the lob over the backhand side for greater success.

Subjects for Doubles Play

- **How to use the advanced positions of doubles play.** The positions change a little from the positions of beginning tennis players. The net players move farther away from the net, at the start of the point, but move in and out with the exchange of the rallies. The players also move more toward the middle of the service box to share the responsibilities to cover the middle of the court.

- **How to communicate in doubles.** Use signs with each other to decide where to place the serve or return, the decision to poach or not, and in what direction you are going to move after the serve or return.

- **How to play the low return at the feet** of the serve and volley player. With the use of spin or slice, the trajectory and speed can be affected with the rotation of the ball to make it dip down to the feet of the opponent.

- **How to play serve and volley.** The key is to teach players what the possibilities are with each target off the serve and return option.

- **How to play the low volley.** Making a decision in playing down the line or cross will depend mostly on the height of the ball and the movement of the opponent.

Andy Murray

Teaching Different Styles of Play

There are many different ways to play tennis, but there are only a few distinguishing styles of play. The style of a player is determined by the method and consistent reproduction of the strokes and patterns. Every player eventually chooses a certain style of play they feel comfortable with. A style of play has to mature over time. It is not something that is often found in beginning tennis players. They might have either an aggressive, neutral, or defensive style of play. It is the task of the coach to assist the player in finding a style that suits their strokes to make them feel comfortable during play and to suit their character and expression of the game.

Styles of Play

- **The aggressive Baseliner**

This player tries to dominate from the baseline with aggressive baseline strokes in order to get the opponent off balance. They move the opponent around the court using the speed, spin and angles of the ball to draw mistakes from their opponent. They play aggressive in every way: physical, mental, technical, and tactical. The player is quick to move around the court and has a first strike mentality. The qualifications to become an aggressive baseliner are the following:

1. Aggressive nature of play
2. Mental and physical strength
3. Speed with the arms and legs
4. First-strike mentality

Training: The coach will try to assist this player by teaching the basics of the third-ball strategy (also called first-strike strategy) and open-court strategy. The third-ball strategy is the tactic and technical execution of how to play the ball that returns from the opponent after the serve. This first-strike strategy is based on taking advantage of the return by taking time away from the opponent and applying pressure. The open-court strategy is the tactic and execution in keeping the opponent running to draw errors and to not allow them to apply pressure on you. Players with this particular style of play have very strong baseline strokes and like to be in control of the rally. Their footwork is aggressive in nature to fit their strokes. Note: Once this open-court pattern is established, you will have an opportunity to play behind a player and wrong-foot the opponent.

- ## The All-Court Player

This player tries to mix up baseline and net play in order to disrupt the rhythm of the opponent. The all-court player is just as comfortable at the baseline as playing serve and volley or approaching the net. An all-court player can mix up spin and slice and accelerate at any time. Their footwork is very well developed and adaptable to the various tactical situations in playing either offensive or defensive tennis. This player is very good at creating opportunities to pressure the opponent from the baseline or net position. The qualifications for an all-court player are as follows:

1. Technically well-developed strokes
2. Good footwork in offensive and defensive situations
3. Good strategic and tactical insight
4. A creative and adaptable mind-set

Training: The coach will stimulate this creative player in learning all the different strokes and footwork necessary to feel comfortable all over the court. The all-court player will have to spend time practicing offense and defense as well as practicing serve and volley and approaching the net in different situations. The coach has to be very supportive and instill patience since the development of an all-court player takes more time to develop than the other playing styles.

- ## The Defensive Player

This player plays very consistent and tries to run down and return as many balls as possible in order to draw mistakes from the opponent. Often, these players will try to slow down the rallies by playing higher over the net and adding spin. The defensive player has very good footwork and relies much on their speed to track down every ball. They can play topspin as well as slice on their ground strokes. They have a high first-serve percentage to apply pressure. The qualifications for this player are the following:

1. Well-developed ground strokes with topspin and slice
2. Great speed on their footwork
3. Great stamina
4. Mental endurance

Training: The coach will support the player by practicing consistency in the execution of the defensive ground strokes and footwork. As the player becomes more proficient, you can add more topspin and slice. Footwork and fitness are key elements to play this game style. Practice matches are focused on playing defensive and neutralizing patterns to draw mistakes from the opponent or to wear them out physically.

- **The Serve and Volley Player**

This player seeks to go forward behind the serve and volley the ball in order to apply pressure by taking time away from the opponent. The serve and volley player has an aggressive playing style and likes to play fast points. The player has strong legs and great balance and likes to use the volley and speed of the footwork to dominate the opponent. The first and second serve are key elements in supporting this style of play. Most often, the player will have the same aggressive nature in the return games and try to seek the net position. The qualifications for this particular player are the following:

1. Good serve and volley development
2. Fast and agile footwork
3. Aggressive ground strokes to force a short return
4. Aggressive nature in playing the game

Training: The coach will assist in the practice of the serve and volley techniques and aggressive ground strokes. The coach has to guide the player through all the target and response possibilities for players to fully comprehend and recognize the serve and volley patterns. This style of play takes a lot of time to develop and is not suitable for beginners. It is possible to practice a lot of approach games to hone the skills for later in their development.

- **The Counterpuncher**

This style of play is for players that use targets to pass the player at the net or to lure them into certain positions and then accelerate the ball to gain the advantage. The counterpuncher has fast and agile footwork and is handy and crafty in creating shots to maneuver the opponent. This player will often leave a certain section of the court open or attempt to bring the opponent into the net when they are not expecting this particular strategy. This strategy is designed to create an element of surprise and distraction that will cause confusion during execution. The counterpuncher will take advantage of the opponent before they are properly prepared and tactically positioned for the offensive. The qualifications for this player are the following:

1. Fast and agile footwork
2. Topspin and slice ground strokes
3. Creative mentality
4. Good touch

Training: The coach will try to create practice sessions where the player has to defend either at the baseline or create a passing shot or lob over the opponent. The key element for players to learn is how to exploit the tactical situation by catching the opponent off guard and taking charge of the situation with rapid action.

Strategy and tactics are comparable with the art of war; you exploit the strengths and weaknesses of the opponent.

PHYSICAL TRAINING

The physical training of tennis players is very diverse. It involves almost all of the muscle groups and requires many physical components. The intense burst of energy during the rallies is alternated with periods of rest. Tennis players use the following physical components:

- Stamina (endurance)
- Coordination
- Strength
- Speed
- Flexibility
- Balance

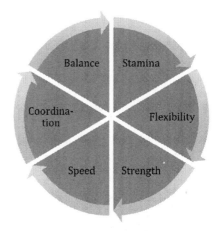

The six components need to work together in the execution of all the strokes. Some of the components have more impact on the physical performance of the player than others. For example, coordination is, by far, the largest component in the development of a player and approximately makes up 60 percent of the physical assets (this might vary between players). To improve the tennis technical aspects of players with specific physical training, you need to understand these components well and train accordingly. The frequency, duration, and intensity of the training are coordinated with the age, experience level, and physical capabilities of the player.

Endurance comes into play when matches start lasting longer than one hour. Since the best-out-of-three-set matches can sometimes last up to three hours or more, competitive players do wise to train this component well. Training endurance for tennis players needs to be specific with the interval of training and rest. Rallies in tennis are usually short, but with junior tennis players, they can last much longer. With a twenty-five-second rest time in between points, the best form of endurance training for starting tennis players is interval training (training units alternated with rest). Start with thirty-minute workouts at first before lengthening the duration.

Example workout 1: - *Three-hundred-yard sprints with thirty-second rest (ten times)*
- *Two-hundred-yard sprints with thirty-second rest (five times)*

Example workout 2: - *Relay runs in groups with a straight course (five times)*
- *Relay runs in groups with change of direction (five times)*

Example workout 3: - *Sprinting eleven doubles sidelines (three times)*
- *Sprinting spider run (three times)*
- *Sprinting twenty-yard dash (five times)*

Coordination is the most important physical component in performing the strokes. It involves the flexing and extending of the muscles to move the body in a smooth and timely fashion. The coordination in striking the ball with the racket at the right time is called timing. The proper coordination and timing controls the correct contact points and trajectories. The other physical components have an effect on how the coordination is performed. In long matches, you can imagine that the strength and stamina will affect the coordination and performance of a tennis player. This is also the case with the other physical components.

Note: When practicing with excessive power, the coordination will be negatively affected. Testing players has proven that with around 60 percent of the maximum power, the coordination of the strokes will decrease (see technique instruction).

Practice: Creating drills with long rallies will train the coordinative skills more than using shorter rallies with too much power involved. Drills with reoccurring and repetitive patterns will have the most effect on coordination and timing.

Strength takes time to develop with beginning players and juniors. The strength is defined by the power of flexing and extending of the muscles in creating movement and strokes. With tennis being a repetitive sport and the matches lasting quite long, the strength is defined by endurance as well.

Note: When training young juniors before puberty, do not use weights. Using weights at this age can affect their physical growth. It is best to use their own body weight or light elastic bands (see practice).

Practice: Instead of practicing strength in a weight room, it is much more appropriate to train this component during tennis training or with tennis specific physical training on or off court. A medicine ball and some light elastic bands are usually sufficient.

Speed is defined by how fast the movement is within a certain time frame. It is made up of several components that determine how fast a player can move: quickness of action, change of direction, and velocity of movement. All can be trained separately or in combining the components together.

- *Quickness of action* refers to how fast the arms and body move during the hitting phase with the ball (fast body action).
- *Change of direction* is the speed of the player in slowing down the movement, turning and running in a different direction.
- *Velocity of movement* is the speed of the player in running from point A to point B.

Some players may not be able to attain every type of speed, but they can all be trained to a certain degree.

Note: For beginning players and juniors, speed is not of great importance yet since most of the ball exchanges are relatively slow.

Practice: It is fairly easy to train all components above with simple games and competition against their peers. An example is to use sprints and competition against each other in teams. The same is possible with change of direction. Train quickness in throwing a light medicine ball in a game of mini tennis in the service boxes. You can speed up the arms by using foam balls or mini tennis balls as practice and point play.

Flexibility of the joints is different for every player. It defines the range of motion of the joints and the elasticity of the muscles and ligaments. It is a component to train on a regular basis to maintain fluidity of motion. Good flexibility comes with some benefits to the tennis player. It provides less friction in the joints and, therefore, less effort in performing the motion.

The strokes will have less effort in endurance and efficiency in the long run. Flexibility can be very beneficial to the speed of movement and hitting. The range of motion, elasticity, and less friction in the joints can all contribute to increasing the speed.

Practice: Flexibility should be a standardized part of the training in the warm-up with dynamic flexibility exercises and with static stretches in a cooldown after the training

Balance is part of every stroke in tennis and provides the stability in motion. Without balance, it would be very hard to coordinate strokes and footwork to hit the ball with any kind of smooth motion. Balance needs to be maintained before, during, and after the stroke for it to be effective at all. If any of these three components is out of sink, it will immediately have a negative result in the execution of the stroke and movement. Coaches should look for these signs during practice and matches since they often indicate a problem that needs attention. This could be the balance of the stroke itself or it could be a deeper lying technical, physical, or even mental issue.

Note: In order to improve the technique, you must first analyze the strokes. The most important things to watch for are the balance before, during, and after the motion in combination with the contact points.

Practice: This component is trained best by working on rhythm drills and improving the technique of the recovery footwork to enhance balance of the strokes.

Physical training has become one of the corner stones in modern tennis.

Justine Henin

MENTAL TRAINING

The mental game is an intricate part of playing tennis. It becomes even more so when playing in competition or tournaments. Some players are already equipped with this toughness and perseverance in wanting to compete and succeed. But to others, it can be their downfall and a struggle to overcome. For many players, this is the toughest part in the tennis game to master. You can see the difference in mental attitude as the players become more competitive and begin to play one another in tournaments. Most players don't knowingly work on their mental ability, but every game introduced to players intrinsically involves a mental aspect to it. It requires the players to push themselves to find an answer to every problem they encounter in the game, may it be technical, tactical, or physical. The manner and forcefulness of their pursuit determines the strength of their mentality. Mental training for beginning tennis players is best trained without the knowledge of the player. When they are less aware and it is introduced as part of a game in order to play better, they will accept it as part of the tactical competition in tennis. This works especially well for young juniors!

Habits

As players progress and become more competitive, mental training should become a part of practice. Starting young players with good habits can have a long-lasting effect on the success of a player. Creating good habits in dealing with playing under pressure and having the proper competitive response to situations has to be taught at an early age. Players usually pick up improper mental responses by copying them from other players. These responses, if not corrected immediately, are very hard to change later on as they become a customary response or a ritual of the player. Following examples of others is common in prepubescent and pubescent kids because of the peer pressure of trying to fit in with everyone else.

Example: Many juniors don't start throwing their racket or having the extreme vocal outbursts until they start playing competitively and notice other juniors doing this. The same goes for girls that grunt excessively during play and copy this from one another.

Rituals

Many rituals are part of the learning process of mental training. They help maintain focus to stay on track with the game plan and execution of the strokes during play. It stimulates the thought patterns to stay calm and alert. When you are distracted or agitated, it adversely affects the quality of play. As a coach, it can be very beneficial to teach these rituals to your players to enhance their focus on the court. As a player, you would do wise to learn these rituals and find out which ones fit with you.

Note: When a player constantly looks to the side for reassurance from the coach or the parents, it will have a negative effect in maintaining the rituals. The same goes for too much attention or coaching from the side. Rituals maintain focus within and maintain the thoughts on the strategy of the match instead of the distracting factors outside of the court.

Mental strength is one the most dominating factors in winning matches and the least trained aspect of the game.

Some Rituals for Beginning Players:

- After finalizing the point, hold the racket in non-dominant hand.
- When missing a ball, walk back to the fence at once.
- Take your time (twenty-five seconds) in between points.
- Towel off between points.
- While getting ready, look at the strings of the racket (maintains focus).
- Think of strategy in preparation for the next point.
- Don't rush the preparation of the serve or return.
- Maintain a good attitude and demeanor throughout the match.

Mental Training Progression for Juniors (maintain attitude and rituals)

1. Play as many games as possible with young players. They love to compete with their peers and will try harder in a game. Use games with and without points to see if players show a difference in mental attitude (this will be a good indication of the mental ability of a player).
2. Play actual matches with normal scoring to see how the player responds to the pressure of a match and competition against their peers.
3. Practice playing with a tactical or mental subject in mind. You can do this for one or both players. This trains the focus and problem-solving aspects.
4. Practice playing under pressure by shortening the game. Starting at 30-all, the intensity will increase considerably!
5. Practice playing points when down in score and up in score. By starting the game score at 0-15, 15-0, 15-30, and 30-15, players can train the focus of playing one point at a time instead of focusing too much on the score.
6. Play the matches starting at 3-all in game score. It will shorten the sets and increase the intensity and pressure. Players will feel the urgency to play more tactically and physically and automatically increase the mental aspects.
7. Play points with tiebreaks. Not only does it teach students to play these better but will train their mental capabilities as well.

Education and Mental Training

Tennis is not an easy sport to play considering all the different strokes, possibilities of patterns, strategies, and the mental aspects involved. To play tennis well takes great focus and discipline in executing. It also requires great mental and physical stamina to endure in long matches and tournaments. To consistently perform well, you have to train the brain as well as the body. Education is a great tool in developing the mental skills necessary for this game. And it never hurts to be a smart tennis player!

Martin van Daalen

NUTRITION

Nutrition is an important factor in the development of a player. Improper nutrition can greatly affect the player's ability to perform. Younger children and beginning tennis players have different nutritional needs than older players or those who are playing competitively. A good balanced diet is the best way to ensure that there is no deficiency of any kind, leading to a lack of performance. See below an example of the consumption of the various nutrition groups:

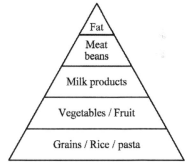

- Carbohydrates
- Fats
- Protein
- Water and electrolytes
- Vitamins and minerals

Carbohydrates are basically sugars. They are broken down with consumption into single sugars units, glucose or fructose, to be used as fuel in working the cells. Good sources of carbohydrates are breads, cereals, rice, pasta, and some fruits and vegetables. Carbohydrate intake does not need to be adjusted when playing occasionally. For competition players, it is more important to eat snacks containing carbs (read carbohydrates) frequently during the day, especially if they play more than one match a day. As a coach or parent, you also need to be aware that players usually don't feel hungry after competition. This can cause problems with multiple matches in one day and the necessary carbohydrate intake needed in between matches.

Fats are necessary in nutrition to provide necessary biological functions in the body as well as storage of energy. The current recommendations for fat intake are 20-30 percent of the daily calorie consumption. Even though fats are important for tennis players, you should try to avoid a high fat consumption just before or during play and keep the intake of saturated fats (butter, coconut oil, lard, etc.) below 10 percent of the daily intake.

Protein is important for recovery and repair of the muscles and body after exercise. This will increase in importance after introducing more weight training. The daily intake of protein should be 10-15 percent of the total daily consumption. Good sources of protein are meat, fish, eggs, beans, milk, etc. With our current diets in the Western world, most of us consume at least that amount every day. There has been an increase of protein intake recorded among athletes with the use of protein bars, protein drinks, etc. This is not necessary for young tennis players and it can be detrimental to their performance. An increased intake of protein has a dehydrating effect that can lead to constipation. Drinking a few glasses of milk during the day will provide plenty of protein for young bodies and is just as valuable as most of the protein supplements you can find today.

Water and electrolytes need to be replaced during competition. During warm and hot conditions, a player can lose a lot of water and electrolytes from sweating. In these conditions, an adult can lose from 1 liter to 3.5 liters per hour in extreme conditions. Windy conditions can also often lead to excessive fluid loss. In these conditions, there is an unnoticeable but constant evaporation of sweat from the skin. Since players don't feel the heat, they don't relate this to thirst and the need to replace the fluid loss. For younger players, the losses might be less, but they can't afford as many fluid losses due to their weight and size. The electrolytes losses from sweating are mostly salt and chloride. Without replacing water and electrolytes, the fluid balance in the body will be affected. This fluid balance is necessary for proper muscle contractions and nerve impulse transmission. The efficiency of the circulation will also be affected due to the blood thickening. This will cause the heart muscle to pump much harder to provide the circulation, which leads to fatigue. Cramps are very common with junior players due to prolonged competition and loss of fluids and electrolytes during play. Hydrating the evening before competition is very important and is often overlooked or neglected. Children will not think of this factor, and coaches and parents can play a crucial role here in educating players in this habit. Plain water is the best to use for hydrating. Drinks containing sugar will keep them awake, and carbonated drinks will have a dehydrating effect. There are many electrolyte replacement drinks on the market today for hydration during matches (Gatorade, PowerAde, and many others). Many of these drinks are relatively high in sugar content and can be watered down or consumed in combination with water to dilute the content during

Martin van Daalen

play. This will maintain a balanced blood sugar and to prevent a sugar high and the inevitable sugar low afterward.

Vitamins and minerals are organic and inorganic substances needed for the body to function properly. Vitamins are more commonly known, but minerals like iron, calcium, or zinc are just as important for an optimal body function. There are recommended daily allowances of vitamins and minerals that should be consumed each day. Eating a healthy, balanced diet (see food group pyramid) will provide many of the necessary vitamins and minerals their body needs. Educating kids to eat more vegetables and fruit and to drink more milk is always a challenge in modern diets but will definitely play an important role in building their bodies and minds. With playing many matches and tournaments, it can be beneficial to supplement the body with vitamins and minerals to ensure the body is not running low on any of these substances. Taking too many different supplements in high doses is not necessary, and they mostly get flushed out of the body anyway. Taking a good multivitamin with a broad spectrum of vitamins and minerals each day will prevent many problems of depletion and support good health in general.

Recommendations for Food and Drinks during Match Play

Good examples of foods to eat during match play are bananas and energy bars. I would not recommend eating other fruits like apples or oranges during the match since they might upset the stomach. Bananas, however, are considered by most players a good source of energy while playing. Energy bars come in various forms. Try to find one with more carbohydrates and less sugar and protein that suits you during play. Drink plenty of water with some electrolytes (see above).

TIPS FOR PARENT COACHES

Training your own kids is not a task to be taken lightly. Kids react differently to a parent than to a coach who is not related to them. Sometimes it works and sometimes it doesn't. The chemistry and communication between parent and child are important, but not the only factors to make this work. If you have the best interest of your child at heart, you will ask yourself if you are the best person to be the coach. Will it help the development of your child, or will it hold them back? Are you experienced enough to help them as a coach? How will being my child's coach affect our relationship? But the most important question of all is, Does my child want me as their coach or is it my wish, as a parent, to be their coach? Most often, your child just wants you to be their father or mother and support them in their sport. I have seen some parent-child coaching relationships work well, but I would urge you to consider all the aspects:

1. *Are you an experienced coach?*
   If coaching tennis is your profession, it can be an entirely different situation than coaching your child without prior experience or training. As a parent, you want the best for your children. If your son or daughter wanted to become a doctor, you would not teach your child about medicine but would advise them to go to college to be taught by trained professionals. The same goes for any other profession. If coaching is your profession, you have the knowledge and the experience to guide your child and teach them proper strokes. But just like teachers in elementary school through college, there are many levels of coaching in tennis. When looking for the best coaching for your child, you need to think the same way.

2. *Are you the best coach for your child?*
   Knowing your own strengths and weaknesses is important for anyone. As a parent, you need to ask yourself: "Am I the best coach for my child?" You need to consider the relationship you have with your son or daughter and how they would respond to instruction from you. Do they take instruction well, or do they become agitated? If you are an experienced player, they might respect what you have to say, but

that does not mean you are a good coach or the right coach for them. How emotional are you as a coach? Emotions can run high when your passion and expectations during practice and competition are higher than those of your child. How experienced am I as a coach? Is it the level of expertise that they need for their level of competition? Put your child's interest above yours to make the right decision!

3. *Does my child want me as their coach?*
Coaching your child should be a joint decision between you and your child. It is especially important for them to be involved in the decision of choosing their coach as they become older and more experienced. No matter if you are a professional coach or a good player, it is still their game, not yours, that needs to be considered. Don't be afraid to ask them what they want and push them to take responsibility in the decision.

Coaching a player requires the coach to emotionally distance himself or herself from the results of the students in practice and competition.

Coaching a player requires the coach to know their coaching experience and their own limitations.

Coaching Your Child

I have observed many situations with parents coaching their child. I would like to give you some examples of the difficulties that arise:

When practicing with other players, it is difficult not to favor your own child by giving them more attention and instruction. If you give too much attention to the other players, your own child will feel uncomfortable. If you give too little attention, your child feels you are neglecting them. It becomes a very delicate balance that can easily be taken the wrong way. When playing matches, it is almost impossible as a parent not to favor your child in their accomplishments. It becomes difficult to stay unemotional during the match and to keep your demeanor in check. Your emotions will often betray you, and your child will respond by becoming more emotional as well.

Teaching on-court etiquette and sportsmanship is a task of the coach. Someone who is not related to the player can do this in an objective and unemotional way. A good coach will make sure the player conforms to the proper attitude to avoid troublesome behaviors as they get older. Parents need to support the coach in teaching the children good behavior on and off court. To be successful as a coach, you can never reward winning above attitude and behavior. As a parent-coach, it can become a difficult ordeal to stay objective. And in some cases, parents don't deal with it strict enough and early enough to fully get it under control.

Note: There have been some classical examples from top players you might know with these problems as a junior. Both Bjorn Borg and Roger Federer had bad tempers and attitudes on court as juniors. The parents had them stop playing tennis for a while. For everyone that follows tennis closely, the results were evident. They became role models in decorum and sportsmanship! These are examples where parents had a positive role and effect on their child as a player.

When discussing matches afterward, it is important to have a clear and concise exchange of information with the player. The objective is to use the information from the match to confirm the things that went well and to discuss how to improve the things that didn't go well. As parents, it can be a difficult procedure to have the same exchange that an experienced coach would have. Emotions, good and bad, hinder a clear vision for improvements. Too many voices fade out the information they need to hear. Even with the best intentions and having everyone on the same page, it still is a daunting task for a player to stay focused on the task at hand. So the key to good development and enjoyment of the game is to have one voice. May it be the parent or a coach, but preferably not both!

Passion for the sport develops over time. It is a feeling that grows from within. It becomes something you look forward to doing all the time, may it be practice or playing matches. There is a pride in the effort and accomplishments. I have seen passion disappear in a player when parents live through the accomplishments of their son or daughter. They start making all the decisions the player needs to make for herself or himself. Getting overexcited about your child's achievements and making suggestions how to play or what to think confuses the player. Parents need to be the grounding force in this relationship. They need to encourage their child without glorifying everything they do. Give your child the space and time to enjoy their own accomplishments. By making it their game, and not yours, you will enhance their passion for the game and their confidence in themselves.

Tournament play and team tennis is supposed to be an enjoyable experience. With kids competing against one another, there is rarely a problem. The problem arises with what they hear around them. Statements made about whom they should be able to beat or how this player does this or that or that he or she cheats do not help the spirit of competition. Parents need to keep their emotions in check by taking the "high road" and not indulging in any form of gossip or speculations. Kids need to experience the tennis game with their own eyes and ears.

Tips for Parents

1. If you are not an experienced coach, have your child coached by a professional. Your child will enjoy you as a parent all the more!
2. Grant children the pleasure to experience the sport for themselves and let them evolve to their potential.
3. Try not to interfere by giving unsolicited advice. Though it might be with the best intentions, it might not be the best advice for them. Encouragement is most often all they desire from a parent.
4. Let your children make their own decisions about tournaments, coaches, training, etc. This will build their confidence in taking charge of their game.
5. Give them time and space to build relationships with their peers. These relationships are an important reason they play the sport.
6. Try not to talk too much about their match unless they ask you about it themselves.
7. Let it be their sport to play. Pride is natural, but let their accomplishments be theirs and not yours.
8. Not unlike other things in life, if at any time you have doubts about coaching your child, you probably should not do it!

Parents are the educators in life and should show by example.

Martina Hingis

PROBLEM SOLVING

Error detection is possible by analyzing the *key positions* of the strokes (see chapters on key positions). By analyzing the key positions separately, with the naked eye or with the help from video, some conclusions can be made to the quality of the stroke. Look first at the key positions of the contact points. (It is impossible to make good error detection without the knowledge of the player's regular contact point.) If this contact point is unstable, correct this problem first before looking at anything else. There is a possibility that there are several technical errors to detect, so even if you find one error, be sure to continue to analyze all positions for other possible errors. Be advised that one error can lead to several other errors in technical execution.

The Forehand

This particular stroke is generally the stroke of choice to most players. Over time, it has the possibility to become a weapon to dominate the rallies, especially with top players. With this in mind, it is essential to develop good fundamentals of the forehand. Guiding players through this stage of development to avoid some of the problems that can occur is an important task for the coach.

Common Errors of the Forehand

- **The Contact Point**
  The impact point of the forehand is a key position in the stroke production. By looking at the contact point first, it gives you a very good indication if all the components of the stroke are coordinated to make a consistent impact with the ball. You will be able to see if the feet are lined up appropriately, if the hips and shoulders are in the right position, and if the arms and racket are in the right position at contact (see figure of player, viewed from above).

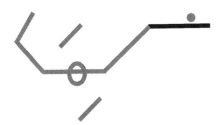

- Contact point at the front foot.
- Balance arm bent at contact
- Shoulder position straight
- Weight transfer to front foot
- Feet position slightly open

- **Movement and Positioning of the Feet**
  Proper timing of the split step and moving the feet behind the ball in a timely manner will increase the quality and consistency of the stroke. The slightly open stance of the feet accommodates the rotation forward, toward the ball. The timing of the split step is synchronized to the opponent striking the ball. The preparations and positioning of the body are essential for proper contact points, balance, and consistency with the forehand.

- **Arms and Shoulder Action**
  The hips and shoulders rotate in coordination with the arms. The balance arm is outstretched on the same side to maintain balance and windup to the stroke. With the push and unloading of the feet, the forward swing is set into motion and the balance arm swings forward and around to finally bend and accelerate the rotation of the shoulders and the arms. The shoulders square off with the racket at impact to produce the maximum transfer of power from the rotation and weight transfer.

- **Follow Through**
  This part of the stroke, right after impact with the ball, has two functions. The first one is to control the acceleration and direction to the ball. Most mistakes of the follow trough lie in the deceleration of the racket head after impact with the ball. By slowing the racket head down, the mass (speed × weight) of the racket will be less. The result will be less stability and control of the racket head against the speed and weight of the ball. The trajectory of the ball will be affected with just a slight off-center hit. The second function is the finish and deceleration at the end of the stroke without any sudden stop. This maintains control and stability to the racket and balance of the body

Martin van Daalen

through impact with the ball. A smooth finish to the stroke will have a positive result on the consistency and execution.

Error Detection

- The player has late preparation before striking the ball.
- The ball goes in a different direction and trajectory than intended.
- The ball is struck at the side of the body instead of in front.
- The ball is struck too high or too far away from the body.
- The balance arm is still on the same side as the hitting arm at contact.
- The hitting arm is bent at contact.
- The shoulders are not square with the racket at contact.
- The knees did not turn forward in the hitting direction.
- The arm and shoulders do not turn forward and square off with the direction.
- The stance of the feet is still closed or crossed over after the finish.
- The player loses balance before, during, or after the shot.
- The player has an unstable and erratic follow through.

Corrections

Making corrections to the stroke is not only about making changes in technique. The cause could lie in a physical, tactical, or mental aspect that leads to a technical change. An example: A player tries to hit down the line and hesitates a little and the ball flies in the net. Here are several examples of the mistakes that could cause this to happen.

1. Choosing the wrong shot to hit down the line (tactical)
2. Not accelerating through the ball at impact and follow through (physical)
3. Preparing too late with the feet and racket and hitting the ball too late (technical)
4. Hesitation that leads to anxiety in hitting the ball with less follow through (mental)

1. Try the whole stroke method first in correcting the stroke. Instead of breaking the stroke down in parts, it can be useful to try it as a whole

first. Practice of the complete motion assists with the rhythm, timing, and fluidity of the stroke. With this whole-stroke approach, you can instruct the students to focus on the follow through. This often will correct many mistakes in timing of the contact points, acceleration through the ball, and stability and control of the racket head.

2. The contact point is the first aspect to look at for errors. For students that often hit the ball late at impact, I use the correction: "Reach more in front to make contact." Other expressions to use are "Keep the ball in front of your feet," "Hit the ball earlier," or "Rotate the shoulders more forward." It is the start of the forward swing (timing), which is key to making contact in front of the body at the correct height and distance to the body.

3. The preparation (movement) and positioning (stance) of the feet are important factors in making good contact with the ball. If, for instance, the feet are in a closed crossed-over position, it is almost impossible to make good contact out in front of the body. This position of the feet hampers the rotation in turning the back shoulder forward to a square position with the ball. The correction to this problem is making sure to place the back foot first and aligning the front foot in the hitting direction. Teaching your players to use this type of footwork in the beginning will enhance the footwork in general and the positioning of the body with the proper stance. As players evolve, they can learn to use an open stance as well.

4. The position of the shoulders is a good indication of the contact point from the forehand. With a semi-western or western grip, used by most beginning players, the shoulders and racket should be square at impact with the ball. Instruct the students to stand with their front foot close against the fence and then reach in front to feel the nails of the hand touch the fence. This gives them a good indication how far they need to reach in front to square off the shoulders parallel with the racket. A method for beginners to use during play is to block the ball and bounce the ball slightly upward at contact to then play it forward again. Slowing the rallies down is a good method to give students time to feel the contact point.

5. The follow through and finish of the action is a telltale sign of the quality and execution of the stroke. The follow through needs to finish by catching the racket in the other hand above the other shoulder. The back leg turns forward, and the foot should finish on the top of the toe. Having your students stop and take a look where they finish can be helpful for them to realize how far the finish of the stroke needs to be completed.

6. Maintaining balance before, during, and after the stroke is imperative in controlling the ball. An indication of good balance is when students hold the stroke in a pose for a few seconds at the finish of the follow through (see point 5). If any technical errors are made during the stroke, the balance will be affected. This method shows the player the quality of the stroke with immediate feedback.

The Backhand

This stroke was formerly taught as a one-handed stroke. With the introduction of the tennis game to younger children, two hands were needed for more strength to perform this action (especially before junior rackets were introduced). Although balance can sometimes be compromised, it is possible to hit the double-handed backhand with more power and control. There are many great examples of players to whom the double-handed backhand has become a weapon that is used very effectively in competition. One-handed backhands should still be taught to players who exhibit an affinity to this stroke and are strong enough to perform the action. For some players, it feels more natural to hit with one hand than it does to use both and vice versa.

Common Errors of the Backhand

- **Movement and Position of the Feet**
  Late preparation in moving behind the ball and crossing the feet over too much are common errors with the backhand. In this sideways position of the feet, the hips and shoulders cannot rotate forward much and weight transfer to the ball will be limited. The balance during and after the swing can easily be compromised. The position of the feet needs to be organized in placing the back foot first in order to place the front foot forward in the direction of the ball.

- **The Shoulder Position and Grips**

  The shoulder position at contact point with the ball is dependent on the backhand grip. Using two hands, with the backhand, can lead the player to slide the front hand more toward a forehand grip. This can result in a late contact point, difficulty in rotating the hips and shoulders, and a problematic follow through. With a continental grip from the right hand (right-handed player), the contact point will move more to the side of the body than with a full backhand grip. The best grips are formed when the left hand is placed on the racket after the grip is established with the right hand. In this position, the shoulders will slightly open toward impact to provide power behind the ball. By using a full backhand grip, the contact points will move more to the front foot and rotation of the body is greatly increased. This enhances the balance, weight transfer, power, and control of the stroke (see figure position below, shown from above).

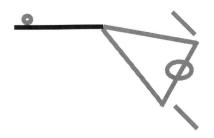

  - *Contact point at front foot*
  - *Arms and shoulders form a triangle at contact point*
  - *Feet are turned forward in the direction of the ball*
  - *Hips turn forward*

- **The Differences with a One-Handed Backhand**

  The shoulders are able to rotate farther backward with a one-handed swing. The swing is initiated with the forward turn of the front shoulder to accelerate the racket. Most problems arise while trying to hit the ball with the hand rather than using the knees and swinging from the hips and shoulders. The contact point will be more in front with a one-handed backhand. To accommodate this contact point in front, the grip needs to be a full backhand grip. (You can practice the proper grip by bouncing the ball up on the racket at shoulder height.) The balance arm releases from the racket at the end of the backswing and stays behind in a bent position. Beginning players might experience some difficulty using one hand with the execution of the follow through. You can correct this by using both hands on the racket to teach them the swing path and the proper finish over the other shoulder.

Martin van Daalen

- **The Follow Through**

  The arms are extended forward and around the body. The elbows bend in unison, and the hands finish over the other shoulder with the butt cap facing the target. Using two hands can be problematic for the balance during and after the follow through if the contact point is chosen incorrectly and/or if the follow through is not completed. Both of these instances could cause the player to lose balance during the follow through. An incorrect grip with the backhand will result in a blocked follow through. The hips and shoulders will not sufficiently rotate forward, and the hands will flip forward, through contact, with a loss of control. The arms will be limited to extend forward and follow through over the other shoulder. A completed follow through maintains balance, consistency, and control of the backhand.

Error Detection

- The ball is struck at the side of the body.
- The player has late preparation with the movement and/or the split step.
- The placement of the feet is sideways.
- The feet are too far apart and crossed over.
- The back arm is bent at the elbow at contact.
- The shoulder position is closed at contact.
- The body loses balance before, during, or after the stroke.
- The back wrist flips through at contact.
- The follow through is erratic and unstable.
- The shoulders do not rotate and square off with the direction.
- The hands did not finish over the other shoulder.

Corrections

Making corrections to the backhand is relatively easy in comparison with the forehand. This is because of the mechanics of the body with the position of the main shoulder of the backhand being in front. With the forehand, the shoulders have to rotate forward first before the arm can swing forward. With the front shoulder already in position, the backhand has one less link to make and simplifies the action and impact with the ball.

1. Try the whole method first and instruct the students to focus on making a full swing with a full follow through. By making the whole motion, the swing will smooth out and facilitate the rotation of the hips and shoulders. In turn, this will assist in hitting the contact point out in front of the body. If the stroke production is still problematic, look for errors in the key positions. Start by checking the contact point first.

2. The contact point differs between one-handed and two-handed backhands. It is generally slightly more in front of the body, for a one-handed player, but this depends on the grips used with both strokes. In both cases, players should strive to make contact with the ball at or just in front of the front foot.

3. The positioning of the feet is of great influence in executing the stroke. The mistakes mostly lie in the direction of the front foot and the setup of the feet. By positioning the back foot first and then stepping in toward the hitting direction, the weight transfer and rotation toward the ball are greatly enhanced. Most beginning players will start by stepping with the front foot first and get stuck in a sideways position. The position of the front foot needs to be at a forty-five-degree angle to the body in order to ease the forward rotation and release of the hips and shoulders.

4. The positioning of the shoulders at impact is crucial to the power transfer from the legs, hips, shoulders, and arms to the racket. The shoulders are slightly open at impact. (For the double-handed backhand, this will be more so that the back arm can drive through the ball at impact.) You can practice this position by instructing the players to stand with their front toe against the fence. With the racket parallel to the ground, have them reach and touch the fence in front. It will provide the students some feedback of how the shoulder position should be at contact. Another method is to block the ball slightly upward at impact point and hit the ball back to the other side. Playing tennis in slow motion is another technique used to teach the proper contact point.

5. The follow through needs to be extended forward and upward with the elbows to bend at the end of the extension over the other shoulder. Most errors in the follow through are caused by not completing the follow through and/or squeezing too hard on the grip. Double-handed

Martin van Daalen

players often don't keep the elbows together and spread them too far on the follow through. Spreading the elbows will not keep the racket head in the hitting direction. The arms need to follow the direction of the ball for the hands to meet above the other shoulder. Finish with the butt cap of the racket in the hitting direction. To provide a smoother follow through, players can practice to release the muscles in the hand by extending the fingers at the end of the follow through. Another method is to have the player stop at the end of the stroke to see if they did the follow through correctly.

6. Maintaining balance throughout the stroke is important for power and control. If the balance of the player or stroke is disturbed before, during, or after completion, the outcome will be less predictable. The body will automatically try to restore the balance by compensating with sudden recovery movements, resulting in unexpected trajectories of the ball. A great balance exercise is to hold the stroke at the end and pose for a second or two. You can perform this either with or without the recovery footwork. *Without the recovery*—the weight needs to stay on the front foot and the back foot turns to the top of the toe. Proper technique is required to maintain the balance before, during, and after the backhand stroke. *With recovery*—after the stroke is performed, the feet have squared off with the student maintaining balance for two or three seconds before moving back to the starting position. This drill will give both player and coach an opportunity to verify the execution and provide some feedback to the quality of the stroke.

Novak Djokovic

The Service

The service action requires the most coordination of all the strokes. With the arm tossing the ball, the knees bending, shoulders rotating, and the racket arm swinging back into a striking position, these motions all have to synchronize together to produce a balanced motion. The service action is the first stroke to start a point in competition. In teaching this action, it will be favorable to break it down in pieces before trying the whole motion at once. At first, teach the toss of the ball separately before practicing the toss and backswing together. Next should be the practice of striking the ball with the racket in a ready position over the shoulder. After mastering all the motions separately, the students can attempt to combine them all together.

Common Errors of the Serve

- **Bad Toss of the Ball**
  Tossing the ball consistently into the same striking position is more difficult than it looks. The ball needs to be at the right height, straight up from the hand and slightly right of the body. If you go by the numbers on a clock, you would toss the ball at one o'clock. To obtain more consistency and accuracy to the toss, train your students to straighten both arms at the start of the toss and swing them downward together and up to a figure Y position. When tossing the ball, flex the wrist downward with the palm of the hand turned open. Use two balls in the tossing hand. This will ensure that students are using the correct grip on the ball with the tops of the thumb, the index finger, and the middle finger. The ring finger holding the second ball is there for support only.

Ana Ivanovic
In this picture, Ana Ivanovic, as a young child, demonstrates a typical example of a ready position of a beginning player. As you can see, both arms are bent at the elbow. The

racket is turned inward by the wrist. The ball is held with all the fingers in the palm of the hand instead at the top of the fingers. Teaching kids the correct way from the start can prevent problems at a later stage. I have seen professional players who have trouble tossing the ball under pressure. Is it a coincidence, or is it related to how they were taught as a junior? That is hard to say without knowing all the facts, but it is a possibility.

- **The Backswing**
  The backswing of the service action needs to be a relaxed, smooth motion in coordination with the arm tossing the ball. With professional players, this coordination between the two arms can vary, but with beginners, we should try to make this stroke as easy as possible. Turn the position of the feet slightly sideways in the direction of the right net post (right-handed player). This accommodates the rotation of the shoulders and the tossing arm to be in the correct position when releasing the ball (see figure below). Many beginning players have trouble in coordinating the backswing with the tossing arm. The backswing becomes erratic and often bends at the elbow before reaching the top of the backswing.

The service action, demonstrated on the left, shows how the arms move upward together. Both arms are relaxed. The wrist is flexed to enable the straight release of the ball (watch the finger positions on the toss to ensure the direction of the ball). The feet are placed in a sideways position, with the left foot slightly in front of the right foot. This position enables the rotation of the shoulders and the position of the toss out in front. With beginning players it can be very instrumental to have both arms up in a Y position to keep the elbow up.

Martin van Daalen

- **Hitting Action**
  With beginning players, there is little knee action involved in hitting the ball. Therefore, the action starts with the unloading and release of the rotation from the shoulders upward and around to strike the ball. Trying to hit too hard and collapsing the body before impact are common errors. Other errors are making contact with the ball at too low a point in the toss and changing the grip to accommodate the contact point. Maintaining a good posture during execution and finishing with the back foot on the top of the toe ensures more balance and consistency in producing the service action. The tossing arm becomes the balance arm after the toss. Making sure the students hold the position of the toss as long as possible makes for better balance and posture. The balance arm then drops to the trunk area to enable them to catch the racket at the finish of the stroke.

Error Detection

- The arms are bent at the starting position.
- The arms do not move together to reach the Y position.
- The elbows bend too early during the motion.
- The body sways during the backswing.
- The shoulders are straight (ninety degrees) with the baseline.
- The elbow of the hitting arm drops too much.
- The toss is too high or too low.
- The ball is struck too far in front of the body.
- The ball is struck as the body bends downward from the waist.
- The player falls over in the follow through.
- The player blocks the follow through.

Corrections

1. Have the player stand next to the fence and hold the racket straight up. The toss should be slightly higher than the racket. The hand should be close to the fence with the ball toss straight upward. Make sure the arm is straight when tossing the ball.

2. Place the racket handle in line with the foot on the ground. Practice the toss by having the ball bounce in the middle of the strings when it returns back down from the toss. Try this also with the

racket already in the hitting position behind the back and later with the backswing added to the Y position. Make sure both arms are straight at the beginning of the backswing motion.

3. Practice hitting the ball after the first two exercises. Start with the racket in the ready position behind the shoulders. With satisfactory results, advance to hitting the ball with the whole swing and the backswing added to the motion.

4. Practice the balance and posture of the service action by finishing the stroke and holding the position at the end. The back foot finishes on the top of the toe with the heel up off the ground. The back knee faces forward.

5. Practice with targets in the service boxes. This will give the students a good indication where to toss the ball. If the ball goes long, the toss is usually too far back. If the ball goes in the net, the toss is usually too far forward *(note: besides the depth, the toss will also affect the direction of the ball)*.

6. Once the knees come into the action, have the players jump and come down on the front foot and hold the position there. The back foot will counteract the momentum of the body and swing upward for balance. Watch that players maintain their posture!

The Volley

The meaning of the word *volley* in tennis is "strike before it lands." The purpose of the volley is to pressure the opponent by hitting the ball in the air and closing to the net before they can reach the next ball. The stroke is executed by flexing the wrist to the side and in front of the body, followed by the step forward against the ball. The angle of the racket should be close to forty-five degrees from horizontal. With the forehand volley, the supporting hand separates from the racket and is kept in front for balance during the stroke. With the backhand volley, the hand stays on the racket during the backswing. The supporting hand separates from the racket during the forward swing and extends in the opposite direction.

Common Errors of the Volley

- **The Grips**

  To achieve maximum control, the grips of the volley need to be adjusted, for each stroke separately, to a continental forehand and continental backhand grip. In the beginning, most players need some time to adjust since the feel of the swing differs from the other strokes. Using the proper grips will position the wrist and the racket in the correct angle at contact point in front of the body. The supporting hand is needed to change grips from forehand to backhand and vice versa.

- **The Backswing**

  Making too big of a backswing and/or not flexing the wrist back in position cause most of the mistakes. The backswing of the volley should start with the flexing of the wrist and keeping the elbow in front of the body. The spacing between the elbow and the body allows the elbow to swing inward when needed and provides power with the contact point out in front. Not unlike other strokes, most players will associate power with a longer backswing. With the volley, however, the power is generated mostly from the legs by stepping into the ball and a short punch from the racket.

- **Contact Point**

  This point can vary according to how far the ball is from the body and the height of the ball. For example, the contact point with the volley is more in front with a low shot in comparison with a volley struck between waist and shoulder height. Many players do not adjust for the height of the ball or have the contact point too far back or at the side of the body. This locks the elbow in the side of the body and restricts the movement of arm and racket.

- **Stepping In**

  The method and timing to step forward and meet the ball are crucial for a good execution of the volley. Beginning tennis players often do not step forward or make the step in far too late. The knees should be in a bent position at contact. Positioning the body on time behind the ball and not reaching across too much with the feet is an important instruction to students. Otherwise, the result will be a longer backswing with too much arm action.

- **Wrist Action**

  The wrist needs to be firm at contact but not constricting in movement. This is a difficult concept for beginning players since they lack time to experiment and gain experience with the touch of the ball. The bottom edge of the racket is slightly under the ball at all times to counteract the downward arc from the ball after passing the net. Many players have trouble controlling the angle of the racket at contact or drop the racket head under the level of the ball. This is especially evident on the backhand volley with young players. They have not yet developed enough strength in the wrist to hold this position firm enough throughout the motion.

Error Detection

- No split step in preparation for movement.
- Late preparation with the backswing.
- Too much arm action before the wrist flex.
- The backswing is too long.
- No step in toward the ball.
- The step in is too late or too small.
- The body is out of balance during the volley.
- No shoulder turn.
- The racket head and/or wrist flips through after contact.
- The balance arm is not in the right place.
- No extension of the hitting arm on the follow through.

Corrections

1. Teach the students the timing of the split steps at the moment the opponent strikes the ball. Having them voice the word *split* at impact with the ball makes them even more aware of the timing and provides some feedback to the coach on the correct timing.

2. At first, teach the students to block the ball with the volley action. It will teach the students the proper wrist angle and to keep the wrist stable after contact for better control of elevation and direction. By

stepping in toward the ball and blocking it out on front, the racket angle is maintained during impact with the ball and the students get a good feel of where impact with the ball needs to be.

3. The blocking of the ball will also teach the students a short backswing with just the wrist flex and the step forward. Another method to teach a short backswing with the volley is by holding the other arm under the elbow of the hitting arm. The arm under the elbow prevents the hitting arm from swinging back and around to the side of the body. The elbow needs to stay in front of the body in case the ball is played at the body. This makes it possible to swing the elbow inside and adjust to the distance and height of the contact point. The flexibility of contact points will be greatly enhanced.

4. Teach the students balance during the volley action by holding the position after contact with the ball. By holding the position for a few seconds before returning to a neutral, ready position, the coach can detect if the technique was performed properly. Without a proper technique, the balance during and after the stroke is almost impossible.

5. Teach the students direction by holding the racket head in the direction of the target. The strings need to face the direction of the target throughout and at the end of the stroke. Most beginning players have trouble maintaining the wrist angle during contact. This is especially true with the backhand. You will notice the wrist collapsing and the racket head dropping after impact with the ball. Start slow before increasing the speed of the ball to strengthen the wrist.

6. Teach the students the difference in obtaining power with the volley compared to the other strokes. The length of the backswing can be detrimental to the timing, power production, and accuracy of the volley. Teach the students to produce more power with the length and the speed of the step forward into the ball. This can be further increased with the speed of the punch and extension of the arms through the contact point.

7. Movement becomes an important factor for adjustment when hitting volleys on the move and with the different heights and directions of the ball. You can teach movement by feeding some balls left and right of the player to see if they use proper footwork to position themselves behind the ball and recover in balance after each shot. The player can play the ball back to one corner or target area. This will help improve movement, direction, and control.

Rafael Nadal (Winner, Les Petits As, 2000)

Martin van Daalen

Rhythm and Timing

The rhythm of the stroke is the pace and tempo of the performed action. The timing is the initial start and speed of the stroke in coordination with the anticipated impact point. Both aspects show themselves as the fluidity of the stroke. They have a great influence on how well the ball is struck with efficiency. Finding the rhythm and timing in a stroke is a process of practice, experimentation, and experience over time. There are some players that have a natural talent for this, and they are usually the fast learners of the game.

Common Errors in Rhythm and Timing

- **Late Preparation**
  This aspect is the most common error with players at every level of play. With novice players, it magnifies the problem even more in creating many other errors. It starts with the timing of the split step or not making one at all. The split step initiates the preparation of the unit turn in combination with the backswing, the movement behind the ball, and setup of the feet. Preparing too late will almost always result in bad timing and rhythm with late hits and unbalanced strokes.

- **Hitting Too Hard**
  This is especially true with young players who like to copy the top players by hitting the ball hard. The problem with hitting too hard is that the player loses consistency and control of the ball. Another side effect of hitting hard is squeezing the racket too much and deforming the stroke. The muscles that should be relaxing in the follow through will lock up and restrict the follow through in acceleration and flexibility. This will negatively affect the rhythm of the stroke and the timing of the ball.

- **Weight Transfer**
  This aspect assists in timing and rhythm of the forward swing. Losing control of the weight transfer by falling backward or sideways is a common error not only reserved for rookie players. Starting the transfer too early makes the body fall and lose balance. Starting the weight transfer too late can have its cause in late preparation, the position

of the feet, or improper timing of the ball with the rotation of the shoulders and the contact point. Using proper weight transfer will enhance rhythm and timing.

- **Mechanical Strokes**
  By breaking down the strokes too much, students will lose fluidity in the motion. They will seem to play very mechanically. Encouraging them to hit as hard as they can will cause problems as well. Hitting too hard will force the player to "muscle" the ball. The coordination and unloading of the hips, shoulders, and arms and releasing the racket gets lost in the process. As a coach, you need to teach your players to accelerate the racket within the boundaries of balance, timing, and control.

Error Detection

- Late preparation with the split step and/or movement.
- The ball is hit too late or too early.
- There are many miss-hit balls.
- The acceleration is jerky in movement.
- The elbow is bent at contact.
- The direction of the ball is not consistent.
- The follow through is not consistent.

Corrections

1. Start practicing the rhythm of the stroke with the timing from the split step. The split step needs to be executed at the impact of the opponent's racket with the ball. The student can learn the timing by saying 1 when the ball is struck by the opponent and 2 when the ball bounces and 3 when they strike the ball themselves. The counting provides the training of rhythm.

2. Slowing things down helps create better timing of the ball. It also makes it easier for a player to learn. As the students become better with the timing, they can speed up the strokes.

3. Having a circular-oval backswing helps promote better timing and rhythm with the strokes. The oval pathway of the racket maintains

Martin van Daalen

the momentum while the acceleration of the racket head is assisted by gravity as both racket and arm(s) drop down into the direction of the forward and upward swing. This oval-shaped backswing is, therefore, the preferred technical instruction.

4. Keeping the same speed, height, and spin to the ball increases the feeling for rhythm and timing. You can imagine that with no variation in tempo and pace, the rhythm and timing also stay the same. Players that try too many different strokes and speeds of the ball will have trouble training these two aspects. Coaches also need to keep this in mind when feeding balls to their pupils.

5. Pay attention to a good warm-up! The warm-up is more important than most people realize. A good physical warm-up, before starting to hit, will loosen up the joints and muscles. This is especially important with any stiffness that has built up from playing the day before. A good warm-up will improve coordination of the muscles and have a positive effect on the rhythm and timing of the strokes.

6. Practice consistency in grooving the strokes. Playing balls back and forth at a medium pace and playing as many balls as possible have a remarkable high impact on a player's confidence. This will result in a relaxation of the strokes that will benefit the rhythm and timing in the process. Teaching your students to groove their strokes in patterns is foundational to the success of any good tennis player.

Footwork

Movement on the court needs to be quick, precise, balanced, and efficient in order to position the body in the correct place to strike the ball. The different directions of movement on the court dictate different footwork. Footwork consists of the following:

- The initiation of movement with the split step
- Moving toward and behind the ball
- Weight transfer during the hitting phase
- Recovery after contact with the ball

Common Errors with Footwork

- **Split Step**

    The split step is the balance point before the start of every movement. This should consist of a bounce on the toes and a wide stance for stability. The bounce should stay close to the ground in order to move as quickly as possible. The feet should be positioned outside the width of the hips to push off in either direction. As soon as contact is made with the ground again, the knees bend to push off in the direction behind the ball.

1. *Making the Split Step Too Late*

    The timing of the split step is crucial for good footwork. Anticipating the stroke from the opponent determines, for a great deal, how fast the players are able to move. This anticipation takes focus in carefully watching the opponent. The knowledge of how the game is played, combined with experience of the pattern possibilities, enhances the anticipation in "reading" the opponents moves. There are many players who are not necessarily fast, in the sense of speed, but still move well on a tennis court due to great anticipation. Learning to anticipate the impact with the ball and slowing down the movement before making the split step are key factors to good footwork. One consolation is that split steps can be taught. Learning to master anticipation, however, depends on insight and talent.

2. *Jumping Too High*

    When introducing the split step, bouncing higher on the toes is acceptable. As the players improve, you need to make them aware that as long as they are in the air and not making contact with the ground, they will not be able to move. Decreasing the height of the bounce will speed up the reaction time to move to the next ball.

3. *The Split Step Is Not Wide Enough*

    In order to push off with the feet, the knees need to be bent with the feet spread at least beyond shoulder width. No matter what direction the players want to move, it has to start with a split step. The strength from the legs and the stability of the body will increase with the width of the stance. There is a point where the feet can be too wide and the knees cannot be effective, but in most cases, the feet are not wide enough and cause ineffective and inefficient footwork.

- **Movement**

   This motion consists of many different ways of positioning the body behind the contact point. Movement can be in many forms including running, skipping, sidestepping, split stepping, and changing direction. Making the motion smooth, quick, and efficient will increase general endurance and the options to play different patterns. Cross-training (playing other sports) can have an important impact on the movement and coordination development of juniors.

1. *Using the Proper Movement*

   With so many different types of footwork, players are often confused about what footwork to use. This hesitation can lead to unbalance during the stroke and loss of control. The type of movement needs to be appropriate for the shot choice, coordination, and timing of the ball. Moving too fast will cause the player to overrun the ball while moving too slow will cause the player to reach for the ball. Finding the right speed and length of the steps and coordinating this with the stroke creates proper balance before, during, and after the shot for optimal control. The practice and repetition of the strokes and movements will increase confidence and consistency.

2. *Positioning of the Feet*

   Once the player has arrived at the ball, decisions need to be made on the placement of the feet in correlation with the trajectory and anticipated impact point of the ball. Choosing the proper stance of the feet is critical for contact point, balance, weight transfer, and control of the ball. Beginners often use the wrong stance by crossing over the feet instead of using an open stance whenever the ball is on the outside of the court. Most often, players make mistakes in footwork by positioning their body at the wrong impact point of the ball. Hitting the ball at too high of a contact point or reaching in front and hitting the ball at too low of a contact point will cause unbalance in the strokes. Unbalanced strokes produce less power and control. Teaching the player to make proper decisions on the type of footwork and the positioning of the feet is an important task for the coach.

3. *Change of Direction*

   To change direction, the feet need to be in the proper position to push the body off in a (different) direction. Organize the placement of the feet beforehand and recover by swinging the feet around with the momentum of the body. Before striking the ball, the organization of the proper stance can be very instrumental to improve the speed and efficiency of the recovery back to a starting position.

- **Weight Transfer**
Proper weight transfer, through impact of the ball, will have a positive effect on the balance of the footwork. The weight transfer will act as a counterbalance to the reaction force from the forward swing and the impact force of the racket against the ball. Standing straight up or even leaning slightly backward will aggravate this falling effect even more. The reaction force of the swing will cause the body to move backward and lose balance during the stroke. Falling sideways, forward, or backward is symptomatic of improper weight transfer and result in a loss of balance and footwork and, ultimately, control of the ball.

- **Recovery**
Footwork recovery is the movement of the feet and body to return to a balanced starting position. The placement of the feet is different before and after contact with the ball. The feet placement before impact with the ball accommodates the balance of the body up to the moment of the swing. As the body uncoils, the feet start pushing upward and are able to shift position with less friction from the ground. After contact with the ball, the feet are placed with the toes in the direction of the ball to push off, back to the starting position. The balance of the body shifts, *after impact with the ball*, in the opposite direction. With a closed stance, the back foot turns on the top of the toe. With the finish from the follow through comes the replacing of the back foot and squaring off the hips, shoulders, and feet in the hitting direction. The push-off of the feet propels the body back to the starting position.

Error Detection

- Slow start to movements.
- Slipping and sliding too frequently.
- Unbalanced before, during, or after the stroke.
- Narrow stance with split steps and recovery footwork.
- Too many closed stances during play.
- The upper body moves before the lower body.

　　　　　Martin van Daalen

- Reaching for the ball too often.
- Improper sliding technique on clay courts.
- Not cutting of the corners on wide ball situations.
- Improper recovery technique and position on the court.

Corrections

1. Instruct your students to move side to side on the baseline. Keep the arms apart in order to clap your hands together at the moment you want your students to make the split step, and immediately move in the opposite direction. You will be able to see clearly how fast the reaction and anticipation of your students is by looking at the feet and time lapse after the clap your hands. This is also possible with front and back movement and combinations thereof.

2. A quick way for students to learn the timing of the split step is by reacting to the timing of the feed. Teach this by feeding a number of balls with the students moving and returning them. Have them call out *split* at the moment of the feed. Try to mix up the direction of the balls as well as the timing of the feed. Your students will need this skill as they play points to adjust to the timing of the balls struck by the opponents.

3. The players can further practice this in a live practice with an opponent by playing back and forth and calling out *split* to make a split step at impact with the ball. The timing of the split step will soon become very clear, and players will be able to move quicker off the mark and gain valuable extra time to set up position to strike the ball with better balance.

4. The narrow stance in the footwork is a dead giveaway to the experience level and skill level of the tennis players. It provides more stability and power to the legs in starting the movement and change of directions by lowering the center of gravity. It is no coincidence that the top producing players all have the wide stance in common. This narrow stance can be corrected by using some light rubber bands tied around the ankles. Instruct the students to keep the tension on the rubber bands as much as possible during play. Another method is to feed very wide balls and have them

use very wide stances to recover. They will learn very quickly how valuable this wide stance is in being able to move more quickly and recovering more smoothly.

5. The balance of the body before, during, and after the swing is important for players to feel in control of their strokes. The balance of the swing often starts with the proper stance in each particular situation. A ball struck in the middle of the court has a different stance than the ball struck out of a corner. With square and semiopen stances, the direction of the feet needs to be coordinated with the hitting direction. The stance is anchored with the back foot first before placing the front foot. Often, beginning tennis players will step across their body and block their own movement, swing, and recovery. An easy method to correct this is to hand-feed balls at the baseline and mixing up the direction of the feed. This method gives the coach the ability to instruct very effectively by providing quick feedback in showing the player how to execute the footwork. The progression would be to feed the ball next and to observe the students closely. You will often find them having more trouble to do this off a feed from larger distance. Continue to alternate the hand-fed balls up close, with the feeds with the racket from the other side of the net, until the footwork becomes similar in execution.

6. The recovery of the body after the swing is one of the most important factors in executing strokes with balance. Squaring off the feet in the hitting direction, after the swing, provides the body with balance. Whenever a player experiences an off-balance situation, they will often not finish the swing and follow through and will likely affect the direction, trajectory, and the spin of the ball. You can correct this by instructing the student to make several side steps to the outside of the court after the ball is struck. This method will teach them to swing the back foot around and regain the balance after the swing. As they become more proficient, they can learn to push back to the middle of the court with side steps.

Footwork in tennis should be fast, precise, agile, balanced, efficient and smooth in movement for it to be effective.

Martin van Daalen

Consistency

Being able to control the ball under any circumstance and as often as possible is a key factor in gaining confidence to play tennis at any level. Consistency can be trained and improved in technical, tactical, mental, or physical aspects. These factors all need to work together in unison in order to establish good results during competition.

Common Errors with Consistency

- **Late Preparation**
  Preparing late with either the footwork or the swing will have a negative effect on the consistency of the player. To remedy this, teach students the importance of the split step immediately followed by the backswing.

  Note: Be aware that the racket does not go all the way back in preparation of the swing. An early backswing can be an advantage only when the swing slows down at the top of the arc until it is time to release the swing forward using gravity to assist the acceleration of the racket.

- **Endurance**
  A breakdown in endurance will adversely affect the consistency of the strokes. Muscle fatigue will result in an inconsistent execution of the stroke and possibly a breakdown in footwork, timing, and contact point. Make sure that players are aware how much the endurance affects the outcome of consistency and train the players accordingly. This is possible by increasing the length of the rallies and indirectly increasing the fitness level.

- **Hitting Too Hard**
  Using too much power with the strokes will hamper the performance with a breakdown in coordination and endurance. If the player uses over 60 percent of the maximum power, the coordination will start to decline. When using exorbitant amounts of power to hit the ball, the endurance of the muscles will very quickly deteriorate. Beginning players like to emulate better players by hitting the ball as hard as they can. It is up to the coach to persuade them to play with control and

efficiency. Slow them down by using points or games and demonstrating the tactical advantage of consistency.

- **Shot Choice**
  During points and match play, the shot choice will have a large impact on the consistency of the player. By choosing a wrong pattern or a low percentage shot, the consistency of the player will decrease.

  Examples: In playing down the line more often than cross-court, the player has to run farther than the opponent due to the enlarged angle possibility with the ball moving beyond the outside lines after the bounce. Playing too low over the net will increase the chance of the ball hitting the net and decrease the level of consistency. Playing too close to the lines will increase the chances of mistakes and reduce the consistency and confidence of the player.

- **Contact Point**
  The relation between contact points and consistency lies in the points of impact in the trajectory from the ball (on the rise, at the highest point, and as the ball drops) and the contact point in relation to the body. You can imagine that hitting the ball on the rise can be more risky in timing than at the highest point of the arc or when the ball drops after the highest point of the trajectory. The contact point distance, in front and at the side of the body, is crucial in making a good, solid, and consistent contact with the ball.

  Note: Beginning players have trouble making contact with the ball at the same point in relation to the body. At first it is important to teach the students to back up behind the ball and make contact with the ball as the ball drops in between the hips and shoulders and make impact with the ball ahead of the front foot. With low bouncing balls, make contact at the highest point. Once they learn these concepts, consistency and confidence will improve.

Martin van Daalen

- **Trajectory**

  The trajectory of the ball is determined by the direction, height over the net, and the speed and spin of the ball. The proper trajectory is important for consistency since it determines where the ball will bounce in the court. The coordination of direction, height, speed, and spin is a matter of experience and training. Train the students to play between two lines strung above the net. It will be as if they are playing through a window above the net (see picture below).

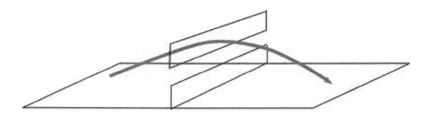

- **Targets**

  The shot choice is the type of shot used with a certain trajectory, speed, rotation of the ball, and a target area. Choosing that target wisely increases your consistency immensely. Hitting the ball up the middle of the court is the largest target possible. Playing cross-court is safer than down the line with the whole court being your margin for error. When playing down the line, make sure to choose plenty of distance from the target to the line (margin for error).

  Note: To play consistently, practice the shot choices by hitting targets areas set up on the court. The best targets are the middle areas of the backcourt behind the service line. You can use flat plastic targets to aim at or use tape to mark the area. You can also use a bicycle tire as a target area.

- **Mental Attitude**

  The mental attitude is just as important for consistency as any other aspect. There are several mental stages a player goes through before stability and confidence becomes reality. Unfortunately, there is no shortcut to success in this area. Some will succeed sooner than others. Achieving consistency in every aspect of the game will portray the mental strength and stamina of the player. The mental stages a player goes through during this effort are as follows:

1. *Surprise*

   After witnessing balls fly out or in the net, the player will be surprised about the results of the efforts. This feeling will gather momentum after seeing more errors occur.

2. **Tentativeness or Blocked Feeling**

   In an effort to achieve more consistency, the initial response will be to become too tentative and not swing at the ball. The racket will decelerate during impact or the player will try to block the ball. The corrections should be focused on making sure the player follows through all the way to the finish of the stroke.

3. *Frustration*

   This feeling of frustration will rise after the efforts do not immediately have an impact with better results. The coach should be encouraging and provide additional help, if needed. Coaching of the mental aspects will help the students to stay calm and persevere in their efforts.

4. *Perseverance*

   It takes effort to achieve results in anything. The perseverance of the player is tested by how much effort they are willing to put forth. This is where a coach can be instrumental by encouraging the player to greater accomplishments. The amount of perseverance shows the passion and desire the player exhibits for their sport.

5. *Feeling of Success*

   Success comes in small doses at first, but it only takes a little success to help the student to try even harder to achieve their goal. This feeling will be confirmed once more practice leads to more success. The coach should confirm the results and reassure the student of being on the right track.

6. *Confidence*

   The more success the player has in practice and competition, the more confidence they will gain. More confidence will lead to further success and accomplishments. The coach needs to confirm how well the student is doing and keep providing positive feedback.

Martin van Daalen

Error Detection

- The ball is often struck outside the "sweet spot" of the strings.
- The ball is often struck late in a forced manner.
- Many unforced errors during practice and/or match play.
- Off balance before, during, or after the swing.
- Late preparation of footwork and backswing.
- The player is trying too hard and swinging too fast.
- The trajectory over the net is too low with little margin for errors.
- The target areas are too close to the line.
- The player is trying many difficult shots.
- The player becomes angry and frustrated.

Corrections

1. Late preparation of the footwork and backswing is the number one culprit of consistency in strokes. The swing has to be executed too fast, and panic will set in. This can often adversely affect the outcome of the stroke and lead to unforced errors. It is possible to correct this by instructing the players to call out *split* when feeding the ball and executing the split step and starting the backswing to a halfway point. They will start timing the ball much better and improve their rhythm.

2. The lack of physical endurance causes fatigue and will often lead to inconsistency. By increasing the length of the rally, the physical and mental endurance will increase automatically. You can instruct the players to play points without hitting any winners. Points can only be won by increasing consistency and endurance. This method is very effective to curtail the players in hitting wild shots. It will also improve the shot choices they make and increase their tactical awareness.

3. The impact point with the ball is important to effectively strike the ball to control the direction, trajectory, and the spin. To improve the timing of the contact point, watch the ball till impact point with the racket. Observing the trajectory of the oncoming ball before **and** after the bounce of the ball becomes an important skill for players to learn. There are several different methods for players the better observe the

trajectory and track the ball to impact point. One method is to write numbers on the ball with a marker and to instruct the students to call off the number before they strike the ball. Another method is to have the students focus on a smaller object than the ball itself. In this case the seams on the ball. Choosing a smaller object will make it easier for them to focus on the ball.

4. The contact point of the ball can be improved by instructing the students to strike the ball out in front of the body. Beginning and intermediate tennis players often struggle to make contact out in front because they don't choose an impact point before striking the ball. They often wait for the ball until it is too late and end up striking the ball at the side of the body. The correction here should be to strike the ball in front of the front foot by predetermining the contact point.

5. The trajectory of the ball over the net can improve the consistency immensely. It not only provides more margins for error but also creates more depth of the stroke in the court. This creates valuable time in setting up properly for the next stroke. This can be achieved by raising the height of the net with the use of a net pole under the middle of the net or by attaching a string over the net as a target to hit across.

6. The target selection on the court will increase the consistency of play. Whenever players try to hit closer to the lines, they will involuntarily squeeze the racket more tightly. This will decrease the timing and coordination and affect the accuracy of their strokes. By using larger target areas, farther away from the side and baseline, they will naturally relax during the execution of the strokes with less chance of unforced errors. The correction here should be to set up target areas with cones, mats, or old tires. This will make them become accustomed to hitting target areas instead of aiming for the lines.

7. The mental attitude will influence the consistency of a player. It is stimulated by success and diminished with failure. Positive attitudes are an extremely important skill for tennis players. Young players struggle with these more than older players, who have more

Martin van Daalen

realistic expectations. Coaches can help players with their attitude by making them aware of the tactical implication and the influence of their attitude on their consistency. This can be done by videotaping them. Review their results with them and reassure them of how consistency can be their friend in winning matches. If you are able to convince them that a positive attitude will improve consistency, then you are ready to move to the next step of achieving better endurance and mental determination to execute. Positive results will lead to improved attitudes and more confidence.

Positive results with consistency creates confidence in playing the game!

Depth

The depth of strokes is controlled by a combination of the trajectory of the ball and the target area on the court. The height over the net will increase the depth of the ball in the court and make the ball flight longer. Speed and spin can change the trajectory and target quite a bit. To hit the ball shorter in the court, the trajectory will be lower over the net and the player has to add spin as the speed of the ball increases.

Common Errors with Depth

- **Trajectory**
  Most often, players will use speed alone to hit the ball deeper. Using more power (speed) causes them to hit with less efficiency and increases the chance of mistakes. This method is not only more risky but also makes the ball flight and bounce much easier for the opponent to strike the ball between hips and shoulders. With angle shots, the errors lie in the height over the net and the amount of spin. Beginning players do not usually possess the skills to execute this shot with consistency, but they still try it often!

- **Target Area**
  When practicing more depth and hitting the ball higher over the net, the trajectory will have a longer ball flight. The deviation of the ball to the left or right can easily be affected by spin or windy weather. Therefore, choosing larger targets with more margins for error becomes

a necessity. Inexperienced players will often aim for the lines and make many unforced errors.

- **Loading**

  Players need to load the muscles in the legs and body to acquire the trajectory over the net. The loading of the legs plays an important part in making sure the racket head can make a low to high swing path in order to direct the ball higher over the net. It also provides an upward push of the body against the ball. The loading of the arms and body assists the circular swing that propels the ball upward over the net. With the higher bounces of the ball, players often don't load the legs to provide the upward swing and end up hitting the ball in the net.

- **Swing Path**

  The trajectory of the ball is largely created by the swing path of the racket head against the ball. The circular oval shape of the backswing ensures the forward swing to start under the ball. Players that have a flat backswing will often swing forward with a flat or downward motion that results in many balls hitting the net.

- **Follow Through**

  In order to execute more depth to the shots, the follow through needs to be higher and extended in length. The rotation of the hips and shoulders plays an important role in extending the arm beyond the contact point to follow the path of the ball. Players who don't follow through have less chance of hitting the ball with consistent depth and will have trouble controlling the direction of the ball.

Error Detection

- The ball is truck off center.
- The ball is struck too late.
- The trajectory of the ball is too low over the net.
- The ball is struck with too much force.
- There is no rotation (spin) on the ball.
- The player loses balance before, during, or after the stroke.
- The weight transfer against the ball is inconsistent.

Martin van Daalen

Corrections

1. Whenever a ball is truck off center, the speed of the ball rapidly decreases due to a significant loss of flexibility from the racket strings. This will greatly affect the depth of the ball. Hitting the ball out in front of the body assists in judging the speed of the oncoming ball. By focusing on the seams of the ball, the tracking of the trajectory of the ball will become easier.

2. Hit the ball higher over the net by making the net higher. This can be accomplished with a net pole under the middle of the net or by stringing a line above the net. After a while, the height over the net will become second nature.

3. Besides making the net higher, set up targets to give students a safe area to play within the lines. This is especially important when playing cross-court rallies where the balls can easily fly outside the sidelines.

4. Whenever a player tries to hit the ball too hard, the hand will squeeze the grip during the swing. This will tighten the muscles and tendons in the forearm and the wrist and flatten the swing path of the racket toward impact with the ball. There will be less height over the net, but less spin on the ball. This can easily cause the ball to fly long beyond the baseline. Players need to learn to accelerate without squeezing the racket too hard.

5. The right amount of spin is needed to control the depth of the ball. To accomplish this, players need to load the body and legs for an easy release of the racket head and to add sufficient spin on the ball. By loading the legs, the swing path will have an upward direction through the ball and assist the trajectory and spin for optimal control.

6. The follow through will have a positive effect on the result of the depth of the ball. Train players to follow through all the way on the forehand and catch the racket with the other hand above the other shoulder. Do the same for the backhand by finishing with both hands above the other shoulder. The student can pause at the

end and check the follow through. As a coach, you can point out certain positions of the arms, elbows, and hands at the end of the stroke.

Direction

The direction of the ball is determined by the impact angle of the strings of the racket with the ball and the direction of the hitting zone. The incoming angle from the ball on the strings and the outgoing angle may not be the same. A good example is the change of direction from a cross-court ball to a down-the-line ball. With no racket head speed, the outgoing angle would be the same as the incoming angle (see figure below).

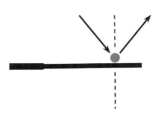

Note: As the speed of the racket increases, the outgoing angle of the ball will change. The deviation of the ball will vary as well with the speed and spin of the oncoming ball into the strings of the racket. The speed of the racket head and the length of the hitting zone will influence the angle (direction) of the ball.

Practice: Train accuracy of direction by hitting between the singles line and the doubles line. It will give your students a good sense of direction and control. Also, practice hitting at certain targets on the court or between targets as an area to aim for. Changing direction from a cross-court rally to a down-the-line shot is still the toughest task at any level of play and needs to be practiced frequently for consistency.

Common Errors with Direction

- **Hitting Zone**
  The hitting zone from a stroke is the area just before impact till just after the contact point. It is an area where the racket almost reaches a straight line through impact with the ball. The length of this area can be increased by the turn of the shoulders through impact. The longer this area, the better you can make contact and direct the ball to a chosen path. Many players have trouble with lengthening this area due to the angle of the shoulders at impact with the ball. The grip can be a dominating factor to the impact angle of the racket with the ball and

Martin van Daalen

can cause restrictions of the hip and shoulder rotation. This will result in the follow through swinging around the body instead of forward

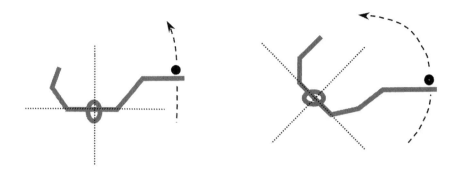

Notice the difference of the shoulder position and direction of the hitting zone!

- **Contact Point**

  The moment of impact with the ball is imperative to hitting the ball straight in a chosen direction. Contacting the ball too early or too late will make the strings of the racket steer the ball in a different direction. Finding the proper contact points is an ongoing quest every time you are playing tennis. There are several different methods you can use to help your students find the correct contact points.

  1. A *proper stance* helps the player to rotate the hips and shoulders and square off the racket at impact with the ball.
  2. The *shoulder position at impact* with the ball is a physical memory point for a player and can assist in extending the racket through the hitting zone.
  3. The *impact point* is a reference point for a player in distance and height while coordinating the timing of the swing with the contact point.
  4. The *timing and rhythm* are critical to the contact point. They are important factors in influencing the consistency and confidence of a player.
  5. The *follow through* is instrumental in assisting players to aim the ball to a certain target by extending the hitting zone and in making corrections to directions.

- **Balance**

  The balance of the body before, during, and after the stroke is important in order to steer the ball in an intended direction. As soon as the balance is disturbed, it will become increasingly difficult to maintain the timing to make impact with the ball and to steady the racket head in the strike zone.

- **Weight Transfer**

  In keeping the weight forward against the ball, the pressure of the racket will assist in stabilizing the racket head and in maintaining the direction on the ball.

- **Follow Through**

  The finish of the stroke after the contact point can be a very valuable tool to make corrections in direction, elevation, and spin. Even though the direction is mainly determined by the contact point, the follow through can help in minor corrections. The player will often learn naturally in making these corrections with the wrist to control racket head angle and trajectory.

Error Detection

- The ball is struck off center.
- Late preparation of footwork and the backswing.
- The player has erratic and wild strokes.
- The balance before, during, or after the swing is disturbed.
- The timing of the ball is inconsistent.
- The player tries to hit too hard.
- Inconsistent contact points.
- The follow through is not complete.
- The racket head decelerates through impact.

Corrections

1. The use of targets is ideal to practice the direction of the strokes. With beginning players, it is advisable to start with larger target areas and slowly decrease the size. By using the large target areas, the players will gain confidence and relax during the execution of

Martin van Daalen

the strokes. The use of targets works especially well in training the direction of the serve.

2. Training of baseline strokes needs to start by learning to play the balls straight down the line and cross-court in the appropriate parts of the court. The next progression is to learn how to change direction by alternating the down the line shots with the cross-court shots. This can be executed by hitting two balls cross-court and to change direction down the line. Repeat the cycle to increase accuracy.

3. A good method to show the accuracy and limitations of the player is by having the players exchange rallies in between the singles line and the doubles line. Players will soon find out how accurate they are with their strokes. It will also provide the coach with an opportunity to work on the various technical aspects to improve the directional control of the player.

4. As soon as the player becomes more proficient in the execution of the strokes, you can limit the size of the target areas and increase the pressure on the control and direction skills.

Mastery of the strokes is demonstrated in the consistency and balance of the swing and footwork.

DRILLS FOR BEGINNERS

Drills are exercises to enhance automatic responses in tactical situations. The coach feeds balls to his students in order to initiate movement and patterns of play.

The drills need to be organized to facilitate what you want to practice or improve with your students. They will eventually, after sufficient repetition, react automatically to similar situations during competitive play. There are several things to consider before introducing drills:

Level of Play

The players need to have enough experience and practice with the strokes before you introduce drills. Repetition of the technique and consistency needs to be established in order to avoid an early breakdown in the stroke production.

Proper Subject

The drills need to be coordinated with the subject matter and the technical, tactical, physical, or mental development of the player. They need to feel a connection with the subject matter, the drill, and their proficiency level before raising intensity.

Progression of Drills

There should always be a progression in the drills from easy to more difficult. Make sure the students have a positive experience to build their confidence before making the drills more complex.

Feeding

The coach can adjust the feed of the ball with speed, direction, spin, and tempo. This will directly influence the response from the player. Adjusting the feed to the level of competency of the player is a matter of practice and experience.

Martin van Daalen

Work and Rest

Drills can be much more strenuous on the players than hitting with each other. It becomes an art form for the coach to correlate the right speed and tempo of the feed, with the movement capabilities of the players. As the intensity increases during the drills, it is important to provide the players with short breaks to recover. Coordinate the intensity of the drill with the effort level of the players by having the drill last for two to five minutes, followed each time with a short break. Another good way to include breaks is to have one player pick up balls while the others are practicing to later rotate back into the drill.

Key to Court Diagram

●	Player Position
▯	Coach Position
○	Target
⟶	Coach Feed
- - ➤	Hitting Direction
- · ->	Player Movement
◄ - ➤	Rally Direction

Drill 1: Baseline Direction Drill

The coach feeds balls to three targets on the baseline. Players move along the baseline and return the feed to the left target. Afterward, players run around and join others at the back. Practice both targets.

Practice: The coach adjusts the speed and frequency of the balls. Students focus on the direction control from different parts of the court.

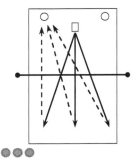

Drill 2: Baseline Direction Drill

The coach feeds the balls from right to left along the baseline. Afterward, they run around and join at the back. Practice both targets.

Practice: The coach adjusts the speed, the frequency, the height, and spin of the ball. Players need to learn how to prepare quickly and play the different angles on the court.

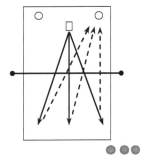

Drill 3: Baseline Direction Drill while Running

The coach feeds two balls. Second ball is fed wider for running forehand. Afterward, they run and join at the back. Students can practice both targets.

Practice: The purpose is to get players accustomed to running down the second ball and returning it in the right direction. The coach can gauge the speed and the direction of the feed to the capabilities of the player.

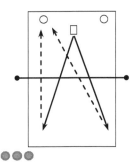

Drill 4: Baseline Direction and Recover Drill

The coach feeds balls to the corners of the court. Players move to return the balls to alternate targets. The students recover to the middle of the court.

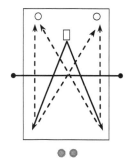

Practice: The purpose is to practice the recovery and movement of the players back to the middle of the court. The combination of movement and accuracy of the strokes is important to construct a point.

Drill 5: Baseline Movement and Rhythm Drill

The coach feeds six to ten balls to the corners of the court. Each student then retrieves the balls and plays two balls cross and two balls down the line.

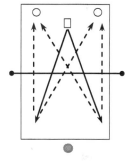

Practice: The purpose is to give the students a rhythm and feel for the rally by running them side to side. The coach can observe movement, balance, ball control, and recovery footwork.

Drill 6: Baseline Consistency during the Rally

The coach feeds the balls to the players on the baseline. They can only play to one side of the court. The one player can play anywhere. Make the rallies as long as possible. This drill is also possible with points.

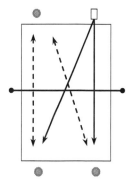

Practice: The purpose is to improve directional control from the two players and to improve consistency with the change of direction from the one player.

Drill 7: Baseline Consistency Two-on-One Play

The coach feeds from the side of the court to the players on the baseline. The players can play freely to each direction. This drill is also possible with points.

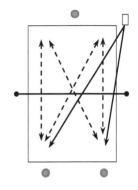

Practice: The purpose is to simulate play against a strong opponent. The coach has influence of speed and angle of the feed in moving the players around the court. As errors occur, the coach feeds in the next ball.

Drill 8: Volley Movement and Direction Drill

The coach feeds to the players at the net. Players step forward to volley. Alternate directions to the targets. The coach can adjust the speed and angle of the feed

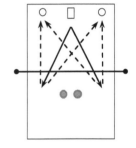

Practice: The purpose is to train movement and direction of the volley. Players should train both forehand and backhand. Recovery footwork becomes essential to the volley.

Drill 9: Volley Direction and Movement

The coach feeds the balls across the court to the net players. They will move continually closer to the net position. The coach can vary the speed and interval of the balls. Practice in both direction.

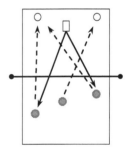

Practice: The purpose is to train "closing the net" with the volley. As players progress, they learn how to close more rapidly in approaching the net.

Martin van Daalen

Drill 10: Volley Poaching Drill

The coach feeds one ball at a time through the middle of the court. Players intercept (poach) the ball as they move across the net. The coach can vary the speed and direction of the feed.

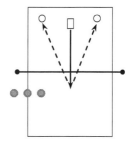

Practice: The purpose is to learn to intercept the ball for doubles play. The players move around and repeat the action from both sides.

Drill 11: Combination Approach Drill

The coach feeds three balls in sequence. Start with a baseline stroke, then an approach shot and a volley to finish. Practice this drill from both sides. The coach can adjust speed, spin, and intensity.

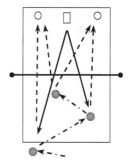

Practice: The purpose is to hit a variety of shots to mimic a match situation or rally in approaching the net. Coaches need to watch for recovery and balance during the execution of this drill.

Drill 12: Approach Shots and Passing Drill

The coach feeds short balls so players can approach the ball down the line. The passing shot can go cross-court or down the line. Coaches can adjust speed, spin, and height of the ball. Play out the point.

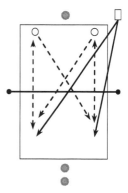

Practice: The purpose is to increase the control and consistency of approaches and passing shots under pressure. Make sure the players maintain consistency.

Drill 13: Two-on-One Volley and Baseline Drill

To start the rally, the coach feeds the ball to the net players. They only return the volley to one side of the court. Coaches can vary speed, angles, and overheads.

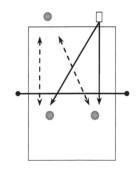

Practice: The purpose of the drill is to train automated responses from the players to rally under pressure. The coach should provide a wide variety of shots and keep the students adjusting to different situation

Drill 14: Two-on-One Volley and Baseline Drill

To start the rally, the coach feeds the ball to the players on the baseline. They only play to one side at the net player. Coaches can vary speed, spin, and direction with the players adjusting to point situations.

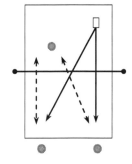

Practice: The purpose of the drill is to train automated responses from the players to rally under pressure. The corrections are made to stroke production and footwork

Drill 15: Two-on-One Volley and Baseline Drill

To start the rally, the coach feeds the ball to the net player. Players can rally the ball around the whole court. Coaches can adjust speed and spin with lobs to create match situations for the students.

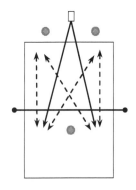

Practice: The purpose of the drill is to train automated responses and movements from the players under pressure. Coaches should watch to see if the players demonstrate recovery, balance, and control.

Drill 16: Two-on-One Volley and Baseline Drill

To start the rally, the coach feeds in the ball to the player at the baseline. The players can play the ball around the whole court. Coaches can vary speed, spin, and depth of the ball

Practice: The purpose of the drill is to train automated responses and movement from players under pressure. Coaches should watch for recovery and control.

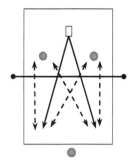

INFO AND WEB PAGES

Coaching Education

Whenever you are interested in teaching or coaching, there are many ways to educate yourself. Some of these ways include books, instructional videos, and coaching education courses. There are tennis education programs available in most every nation. The most extensive of these is a three-year program found in Western Europe. The entrance requirements and exams are very strict, with an average success rate of 60 percent.

The *first year* is for teaching beginners and intermediate players.
The *second year* is for teaching advanced players and team training.
The *third year* is for coaching advanced and pro players individually or as a team

Some countries, like Australia, are expanding the levels of coaching education to five different levels. In the United States, there are several coaching education programs available. The following are the programs that are endorsed by the USTA:

USPTA -- United States Professional Tennis Association
USPTR – United States Professional Tennis Registry
USTA – United States Tennis Association

The PTA and PTR are entry-level coaching education programs that will teach you the basics of tennis and fundamentals of teaching. The PTR has just recently started with an advanced coaching education program. The USTA has a high performance program for coaches with some experience in teaching and coaching and invites coaches for regional seminars. You can find out more about this program by calling the sport science department from the USTA.

There are many other nations that understand the importance of coaching education in order to improve the quality of tennis players. They are constantly researching and enhancing the teaching techniques and methods for coaches and tennis teachers. The nations with great organizational structures in coaches' education, player development, and competitive structure often produce the best players. The ITF (International Tennis Federation) has developed coaching education seminars to share information on the latest developments in teaching tennis. They sometimes offer coaches' training in various countries (mostly to stimulate the tennis in that particular region). This information is available on the ITF website.

Tennis is ever changing and evolving, so it is important for coaches to be aware of the newest trends and training methods. Even the best coach can benefit from a good training program. There will always be exceptional players developed by passionate coaches who take on a mentor role in the development of talented players. But this is the exception and not the rule. So if your desire is to be the best coach you can possibly be, then I strongly encourage you to look for a coaching education program in your country or region. Be willing to learn from other coaches. Seek out the top coaches in your area and study their method and communication of coaching.

Different Coaching Systems

There are different styles of coaching all over the world. The coaching style in Europe is geared toward the development of all-court players who can play on any type of surface. In comparison, the coaching style in the United States and other nations has been more geared to aggressive hard court play. In the last few years, there has been an effort to introduce clay court play more often. For most European countries, the seasons and weather dictate playing indoors for at least half of the year. The surface changes from playing red clay and indoor hard courts and forces players to adapt their game with different strokes, tactics, and styles of play. There is a misconception in countries outside Europe that the level of tennis in Eastern and Western Europe has increased due to more exposure to red clay courts. One aspect to consider is that players have a longer and continuous clay and hard court season to gain more experience on that surface. The fact is, however, that the European countries have heavily invested in their coaches' education and player developmental programs for decades with a systematic long-term plan. Not unlike coaching a player, continuity is required in building a development plan for players and coaches in reaching any level of success. Especially considering that it takes between five and seven years to develop top juniors and even longer in developing world-class players!

Organizational Structure

The structure of federations and clubs is quite different in each country. Most European countries require aspiring coaches to be licensed through a national coaches' education program as opposed to many other countries that require no license or professional training at all. Some countries, such as the United States, offer high school and college tennis programs and sports scholarships for college. In Western Europe, club members are automatically registered as a federation member, which makes it easy to keep track of all tennis players. Most countries require you to join their federation and pay membership fees in order to compete in tournaments. For exceptional talents, you may find special sports schools that offer modified educational programs to allow their students to compete while getting an education. This seems to be more prominent in Western Europe. Though most countries offer a variety of training opportunities, Europe seems to have the advantage due to the fact that their federations are ran in a more businesslike fashion with a long-term plan and continuity of vision.

International Player Development Programs

With young players, the European coaches focus on the development of the basic fundamentals of strokes and footwork. As players mature, they refine and develop the technical and tactical aspects of the specialty shots with topspin, slice, and sidespin. The strategic and mental aspects are trained, from a young age, with on-court coaching during the yearly reoccurring league matches. These club matches with on-court coaching are a valuable tool for young aspiring players in learning strategy and the composure from the older players. The top juniors mature much faster and follow the international schedule in playing a combination of junior and pro events (challengers and futures). Tennis is played in most nations of the world, so it is not unusual that players become used to competing with foreign players on a regular basis. This is an advantage when they begin to play the international circuit.

Martin van Daalen

The Dutch, British, Belgian, Swedish, and German national programs are mostly focused on technical development of the strokes and footwork. Besides the technical development, the French system also adds the attention to patterns of play. Work ethic, footwork, and mental toughness are the focal points of the Spanish system. Many of their players use more spin and their footwork to combat their opponent. Technical development of the strokes is not the strongest factor there. Through some experience in working with the Japanese and other Asian juniors, I would say they are more straightforward in their approach to playing the game. The courts are very fast, and many players play low, hard, and flat over the net with little spin. Speed and first-strike capabilities are dominant among those players. Players are usually not flexible with strategies and will often use the same pattern over and over again. Whatever the system of teaching might be, you can learn a lot just by watching the practice sessions from various coaches. With tennis being the second biggest sport in Europe, after soccer, the athlete pool is extensive in the tennis sport. It is no coincidence to see so many talented tennis players arise from these development programs and dominate the tennis world.

Junior Development Programs

There are many ways to introduce your children to the sport of tennis. If you enjoy playing yourself, you could start by hitting a few balls with your child at a local facility to see if they enjoy it as well. Chances are, they will connect with other young players there and may end up taking some lessons together from the local pro. Check with your neighborhood tennis facility to find out what programs they offer. Most will have something for all ages, such as Quick-Start, mini tennis, and rookie programs. They may also offer training for advanced players. To make a choice on a program totally depends on the motivation and goals of the individual player. Players with high motivation and passion for the sport don't need much encouragement and will push themselves to train more often. The intensity of the workouts will be a telltale sign for parents to invest in training.

Many nations offer various junior development programs for different age-groups and levels. They range from sectional training to regional and national training. In many cases, they have a system in place to coach players regionally when they are younger. As the players progress, they are invited to attend the national training and play on the national team in competition and international events. The national training centers create opportunities for young players to test themselves against more experienced and advanced players. The exchange of experience and the interaction have a stimulating effect in the development of top players.

The USTA offers many programs. There is a talent ID program that identifies young talent in each region. You can check with the section office for dates or player services at the USTA office in Boca Raton. There are junior tennis leagues for the section and districts in your area. You can find information on the USTA website—leagues. There is assistance and guidance available for coaching school tennis. Look for this information on the USTA website—school tennis. There are regional training centers that offer training and camps for the top players from the region. The national training centers for the top players in the nation are located in Boca Raton in Florida, Carson in California, and in New York at the U.S. Open site. The USTA website has much information on all these topics to get yourself started and how to contact local programs. The sections each have their own office to share information on junior and adult programs. You can find the contact numbers and e-mail addresses on the USTA website.

League Tennis

Team tennis has always had an appeal for young and old alike in tennis. There are many leagues available, at various levels, all over the country. Playing singles and doubles together in a team can be a very stimulating, fun experience. There is a website available to find out all you need to know, with directions on how to sign up and what level to play (see "Websites International and in the United States").

Tournaments

There is a wide variety of tournament play available in every country. The federation website can help you find the right tournament information, including dates, level, age, etc. Be aware of the different levels of play available. You can find tournaments for single, double, and mixed play for juniors and adults. Open tournaments are not age related and have an open entry. Make sure you challenge yourself and have some fun doing it. You will enjoy it all the more.

Teaching Tennis and Beyond

This book, *Teaching Tennis*, is the first volume of three books about coaching methodology with a progression of teaching. The first book is focused on the fundamentals of coaching while the second book will be geared toward advanced methods of teaching. Volume 2, *Teaching Advanced Tennis*, will describe in detail all aspects of the game—how to teach specialty strokes and advanced methods of physically training players and how to play the game with strategy and tactics while strengthening the mental part of the game. It also will include many anecdotes on coaching advanced and international pro players during my career as a coach. Volume 3, *Teaching Pro Tennis*, will focus on how to develop a pro player and what it is like to coach on the tour.

You will be able to find all the information about my books on my website. (http://www.xlibris.com/TeachingTennisVol.1.html)

WEBSITES INTERNATIONAL AND IN THE UNITED STATES

A-game.com   http://www.a-game.com
The official website of Smart Athletes helps you play your A game not just in your sport but also in the classroom. It helps you take advantage of opportunities and avoid dangers in sports, school, and life.

ASEP   http://www.asep.com
The American Sports Education Program helps improve the sports program for kids by providing instructional resources, workshops, and courses for administrators, coaches, and parents.

ATP   http://www.atpworldtour.com
Official website of the Association of Professional Tennis Players. It contains various information on players, ranking, tournaments, draws and results, etc.

ETA juniors   http://www.tenniseurope.org
A website from the European Tennis Association. The website contains information on schedules, rankings, draws and results, etc

Human Kinetics   http://www.humankinetics.com
A publishing company that produces innovative and informative products in all sports and physical activities that help people lead healthier and more active lives.

IDTM   http://www.idtm.com
The International Doping Test and Management company provides a service of testing players for doping at competition and unannounced out-of-competition testing for the international sport federations.

IOC   http://www.nodoping.olympic.org
The International Olympic Committee has organized a division that assists in the fight against the use of doping in sports.

ITF   http://www.itftennis.com

The International Tennis Federation is the world governing body for tennis education, tournaments, and international events (Davis Cup, Fed Cup and junior events). This website also provides a junior site.

Junior Tennis.com   http://www.juniortennis.com

An extensive website dedicated to junior tennis in the United States and provides information on international events.

League Tennis in U.S.   http://www.usta.com/LeaguesAnd
                                      Tournaments/AdultLeagues.aspx

This website contains information on all the leagues across the United States in each district. You can get information on how to join and where to play.

NCAA   http://www.ncaa.org

The National Collegiate Athletic Association is an organization of the colleges in the United States that regulates athletic matters at a national level.

NCAA Clearing House   http://www.act.org/ncaa

This organization is the initial eligibility regulatory office that provides public access to approved core courses at high school and other related issues.

Quick Start Tennis   http://www.quickstarttennis.com

This program is designed to introduce young kids to the game of tennis by adjusting the size of the court, rackets, and the balls

Quick Start Gear   http://www.ustashop.com

This website has all the equipment available to start a quick start program. There are nets, rackets, and balls available for each level and size.

STMS   http://www.stms.nl

The *Society for Tennis Medicine and Science* is a newsletter, produced in cooperation with the International Tennis Federation, the ATP, and WTA tour.

Sports Doctor   http://www.sportsdoctor.com

A sports medicine service provided for athletes, doctors, and physical therapists.

USTA   http://www.usta.com
The website for the national governing body of tennis in the United States. You can find any information concerning tournaments, training, results, etc.

USTA Tournaments   http://tennislink.usta.com/tournaments/
                        Schedule/Search.aspx
The official website for all amateur tournaments in the United States. You can find tournament dates, draws, rankings, schedules, and other tournament information.

USPTA   http://www.uspta.org
Official website of the United States Professional Tennis Association. An organization for teaching professionals that provides training and certification for coaches.

USPTR   http://www.ptrtennis.org
The website of the United States Professional Tennis Registry. An international tennis teaching organization that provides an international teaching certification for teaching professionals and coaches.

WTA   http://www.sonyericssonwtatour.com
Official website of the Women's Tennis Association. It contains various information on players, ranking, tournaments, draws and results, etc.

Teaching Tennis   http://www.xlibris.com/TeachingTennisVol.1.html
Official book website. It contains information on the content of the book and how to order.

GLOSSARY

A

Ace — A service winner without the opponent touching the ball

Acceptance list — The list of players accepted into the tournament

Approach — A stroke made in transition to the net

ATP — Association of Tennis Professionals

Auditory — Related to hearing

B

Baseline — The boundary line at the back or end of the court

Backhand — The stroke made with the back of the hand facing forward

Backswing — The part of the stroke in taking the racket back

C

Cross-court — Playing the ball diagonally from corner to corner

Cross-training — Training different sports

Consistency — Constancy in repetition

Contact point — Point of impact with the ball

Court — The playing field

Cutoff — The ranking of the last player accepted in the tournament

D

Double line — Outer sidelines of the court for doubles play

Down the line — The ball is played parallel with the sideline of the court

Draw — A tournament list of players that shows whom they play

Drop shot — A stroke made to stop the ball short behind the net

Drop volley — Volley made to drop short behind the net

E

Entry list	- List of players that entered into the tournament
ETA	- European Tennis Association

F

Fact sheet	- Info sheet with tournament information
Feed	- The ball put in play by hand or with a racket
Forehand	- The stroke made with the palm of the hand facing forward
Forward swing	- The part of the stroke in moving the racket forward
Fundamentals	- The basics elements of the game

G

Groundstroke	- The strokes made with either forehand or backhand
Groove	- To practice with rhythm and consistency

H

Half volley	- Groundstroke made just after the bounce of the ball
Hitting zone	- The area just before and after impact with the ball

I

ITF	- International Tennis Federation
Intrinsic	- Fundamental built-in qualities
Intangibles	- Special, un-trainable aspects of the game
Intuitive	- Known automatically and instinctively

K

Key position	- A recognizable position in the stroke
Kinetic chain	- Sequence of segmental, coordinated, and efficient transfer of energy

L

Loading	- Building a tension and flexibility in the muscles for a stroke
Long line	- Parallel to the sideline

M

Main Draw	- Main event of the tournament

Martin van Daalen

Methodology	- An organized system with a logical order

N

Net pole	- The pole holding up the net
Neutralizing	- The action to counterbalance a tactical situation

O

Overhead	- Stroke made over the shoulder (smash)
Open court	- A part of the court that is not covered by the opponent

P

Periodization	- To plan a training period with a purpose and intensity level
Progression	- A logical order of development
Poach	- To intercept the volley at the net in doubles play

Q

Qualifying	- The event played before the main tournament to gain entry

R

Rally	- An exchange of strokes
Ranking	- The list of players ranked in order of results
Ready position	- A starting position for action
Recovery	- The movement to regain balance and position after striking the ball
Return	- Hitting the ball back to other side in a rally or after the serve

S

Sensory	- Related to feeling the stroke or the ball
Service	- Overhand stroke to start the point
Service winner	- Point won with the serve with the opponent touching the ball
Service box	- Area in which to serve the ball
Service line	- The back line of the service box
Sideline	- The outer line of the court
Sidespin	- The horizontal rotation on the ball

Single line	-	The outer line of the court for singles play
Single sticks	-	The sticks used for the single pole positions
Slice	-	The horizontal (serve) or reverse (groundstroke) rotation of the ball
Smash	-	Stroke made over the shoulder
Style	-	(Personalized) expression of the strokes and in playing the game

T

T	-	The middle of the court between the service boxes
Topspin	-	The forward rotation of the ball
Transition	-	The movement and action from the baseline to the net position

U

USTA	-	United States Tennis Association
Unit turn	-	Rotating together as one motion

V

Visualizing	-	Seeing the action in your mind
Visually	-	Related to seeing
Volley	-	Stroke made by hitting the ball in the air without a bounce

W

WTA	-	Women's Tennis Association

Martin van Daalen

REFERENCES

- *Successful Coaching* (Tennis Edition 1990)
  Rainer Martens

- *Guideline and Training Book for Coaches KNLTB Part A and B* (1995)
  Editor: Frank van Fraayenhoven

- *USA Tennis Parents' Guide* (2001)
  USTA

- *Coaching Different Gender* (2002)
  David C. Gosselin

- *The Power of Concentration*
  Remez Sasson

- *Basic Nutrition for Tennis*
  High Performance Coaching Program Study Guide

- *Playing Tennis in the Heat*
  Dr. Michael Bergeron

- *Nutrition*
  Page Love

- *Sports Psychology Guidebook for Coaches*
  USTA

- *Periodization for Tennis Players* (2008)
  Anne Pankhurst

- *Tennis Recovery* (2010)
  Mark S. Kovacs, Todd S. Ellenbecker, W. Ben Kibler

ACKNOWLEDGMENTS

Foremost, I have to thank my parents for introducing me to this wonderful sport. They have always tried to guide me and encourage me to be the best I can be in whatever I attempted to do. Thanks and appreciation goes to my mother, Joy van Daalen-Scott, for helping me with the editing of most of the material of this book.

Acknowledgment and thanks go out to my two sons, John and Tom, for being the biggest supporters in my career and in writing these books.

I am grateful for all the wonderful coaches who taught me the game. Their teaching has brought out my passion for tennis and instructing others to enjoy the game as much as I have. My thanks go to Mr. van der Berg, Jan Hordijk, and Eric van der Pols for being patient and diligent in teaching me the intricate parts of the tennis game.

In my playing days, there was one person who took an interest in teaching me the tactical and mental aspects of the game. Henk Korteling was a mentor to me, and he was instrumental in teaching me how to control the mind and enjoy the game.

As a student coach, I went through several teaching courses in the Netherlands. There are, however, some coaches who take a special interest in stimulating you to reach higher. Tom de Goede was one of those coaches, and my thanks go to him for pushing me to excel.

This book might never be written without the gentle persuasion of Michelle Axthelm. She has always encouraged me to write, and I am glad I took her advice. She has been a tremendous help and has spent countless hours in the editing of this book. Thanks, Michelle!

Lynne Rolley has been a friend and colleague in coaching and guiding players. She always has been a great support in helping me with players and difficult situations. Her clear vision and experience in management of players, coaches, and parents has been instrumental to me and taught me to look at many different perspectives of coaching and teaching.

Rodney Harmon has always supported me in many ventures and ideas as a coach. He has become a close friend and advisor over the years of working together. I have to thank him for stimulating me to write and create this book of teaching tennis. His passion for tennis instruction, combined with his insight for the game and his positive attitude, has been an inspiration to me. Thanks, Rodney, for the advice, many suggestions, and with the help in editing this book.

Many thanks to the publishing team of Xlibris in taking on this project.

The personal pictures and pictures of the sequences, grips, and footwork are by Martin van Daalen.

The pictures of the young tennis stars are courtesy of Google Images.

The drawings, graphs, and illustrations are by Martin van Daalen.

Martin van Daalen

INDEX

A

B

C

Martin van Daalen

D

E

H

I

J

Martin van Daalen

T

Martin van Daalen

trajectory, 38-39, 43, 63, 72-73, 77, 116-17, 178-79, 204-5, 207-11
transition, 28, 30, 122, 142, 147, 235, 238
trigger finger, 66, 70, 74-75

U

under-grip, 72
unit turn, 195, 238
unloading, 83, 85, 89, 91, 93-94, 97, 100, 103, 105, 109, 111, 178, 189, 196
USPTA (United States Professional Tennis Association), 224, 233
USPTR (United States Professional Tennis Registry), 224, 233
USTA (United States Tennis Association), 7, 13-14, 24, 137, 224, 228, 233, 238-39

V

velocity of movement, 163
video, 49, 58, 127, 130, 177
visualizing, 42, 123, 238
visually, 41, 58, 238
visual training, 49
vitamins, 169, 171. *See also* nutrition
volley, 104-6, 108, 110-12, 126-27, 130-31, 146, 154-55, 159, 190-93, 238
volley and baseline drill, 222-23
volley direction, 220
volley movement, 220
volley poaching, 221

W

warm-up, 49, 52, 139, 164, 197
water, 47, 169-71
weather, 31, 47, 147-48, 209, 225. *See also* lesson plan
weather conditions, 47, 147-48
web pages, 20, 24, 125, 137, 224
websites, 137, 228
weight transfer, 105, 114-17, 178, 181-82, 184, 195, 200
western forehand, 69

Martin van Daalen

Made in the USA
Lexington, KY
13 June 2017